RETENTION MANAGEMENT

The Art of
Keeping, Motivating, Challenging
the Workforce

Subhash C. Puri

Capital Publishing
OTTAWA-NEPEAN, ONTARIO, CANADA

Address all enquiries to:

Capital Publishing
P.O. Box 30051, 250 Greenbank Rd.
Nepean, Ontario, Canada   K2H 1A3
Tel: 613-820-2445;   Fax: 613-820-1739

ISBN 0-9691919-1-X

Cover design by: John Carlo Siewerdt, Brazil

Canadian Cataloguing in Publication Data

Puri, Subhash C.
       Retention Management: the art of keeping, motivating, challenging the workforce

Includes index.
ISBN 0-9691919-1-X

       1. Employee motivation. 2. Job satisfaction. I. Title.
HF5549.P87 1999   658.3'14   C99-900372-0

Printed in Canada

To the three generations ......

To my parents and in-laws,
who taught me the value of learning, and compassion.

To my wife,
who showed me the meaning of life, and living.

To my daughters,
who taught me the significance of love, and togetherness.

CONTENTS

The Prologue

Part 1: The Understanding

Part 2: The Action

FOREWORD

If I am asked to identify the three most important objectives of any business enterprise, I would say, from my experience, that they are: producing high quality products and services, seeking customer satisfaction, and improving business marketability and profitability. Coincidently, the author, Subhash Puri, has also outlined the same three objectives, though in a rather assumingly candid manner: making money, making more money, making more money continuously.

To accomplish these goals, an organization must have: state-of-the-art technology, adequate systems and procedures, and highly skilled and motivated workforce. Technology and systems can be easily acquired or developed, but motivating the workforce presents the biggest challenge. At Marisol, we have tried many motivation enhancement initiatives and programs with varying degrees of success.

But, Mr. Puri's treatment of the subject is almost totally unique and out of the ordinary. His innovative and ground-breaking process of generating motivation through the awakening of the human consciousness and building the human person, has enormous potential and powerful applications. His unique insight and practical approach to solving problems is very well known to us, as we had the opportunity of having him as our external consultant for quality system improvement and productivity enhancement.

Much like his other books, this one also displays Subhash's profound maturity, deep understanding, and his enviable experiential ability to present complex issues in the most simplistic and understandable manner. An author, teacher, and consultant of international recognition and fame, his contributions to the subject are indispensable. I would personally like to congratulate him for his passion, dedication, and superb sense of understanding.

Vicente Donini
President
Marisol S.A. Industria do Vestuario
Jaragua do Sul, S.C., Brazil

PREFACE

"The search for excellence continues . . ."

Human business management is a subject as old as we are, and yet it is as new and challenging as tomorrow. Being the core competency of every business organization, it virtually commands unremitting attention in the overall strategic framework of every organization.

The most predominant issue in human business management is motivation - how to motivate the workforce to improve productivity. Motivation is indeed a complex issue, because it involves a very complex entity - the human person. On top of it, the complexity of the issue keeps increasing as the society grows and evolves.

As if motivating the workforce wasn't enough of a challenge for the organizations in this highly volatile and perpetually changing global environment, today another new and bigger dimension has been added to their operability framework - the problem of retention management - finding and keeping good people for a long-term commitment. Organizations, today, are expending enormous amounts of efforts and resources to find good people, but the rate of losing them to their competitors is becoming even faster. The workforce mobility is almost reaching crisis proportions. Most corporate boardrooms are frantically busy in developing systems and strategies to get a grip on this phenomenon of job mobility. Even the placement agencies and management consultants are shifting their emphasis from helping organizations and/or individuals to locate and fill suitable positions, to helping organizations develop suitable strategies and appropriate infrastructure to keep and retain their already hard-found workforce. The shift in strategy calls for looking inside the organization, identifying potential, and helping and grooming the skills and capabilities of the existing workforce to fulfil the organization's goals - something that is being annotated as *"Retention Management"*.

In this book, we have approached the subject through the most fundamental question: "Why do people change jobs?". A critical analysis of the process of employment and retention is carried out, which reveals that excessive job mobility is a by-product of the worker's job dissatisfaction and general lack of motivation. With this understanding, the book details out a complete appraisal of the goals of the two parties, the management and the worker, and presents some new and unique paradigms of goal compatibility and motivation enhancement.

Since motivation is the main culprit in the human management equation, the book addresses this issue at length, but in a rather unique manner. The usual approach to resolving this dilemma is through building of highly mechanized and regimented systems and superimposing them on the people to motivate them. In such an approach, the emphasis is generally on the system logistics, rather than on the human person, for whom the system is created in the first place. We think that this is inappropriate, and that is why, despite our best intentions and action, our efforts bring only a passing success. We have turned the matter around to defy all the conventional wisdom. We are, instead, making the human person as the nucleus - his/her prowess, potential, drive, and determination - the elements that fuel motivation. Our emphasis is on building the person - tapping the source of motivation - the human psyche - and making awakenings at the consciousness level, so that the individual is self-driven to generate motivation and personal excellence.

Written totally in the human language, the book is meant for the human species. In fact, it is not a book - it is a living, breathing, thinking consciousness. Aimed at the widest possible audience - the human person - whether the person is a worker or a manager - the book is one of its kind in presenting some totally new and path-breaking paradigms of motivation. The book does not fall under one subject area - it simultaneously spans over several fields of study, such as: business management, human management, behavioural psychology, personal development, quality management, etc.

I would now like to make some genuine acknowledgments, and wish to express my profound gratitude to all my friends and colleagues with whom I had the opportunity to work, and whose interaction has provided me with enormous intellectual and experiential wealth, without which this book would not have been a reality. I would like to express my gratitude to at least the following persons: Silvio N. Punchirolli, Rene Paulo Siqueira, Jose Renato Sandrini de Castro, Alexandre Faria, Girogio Rodrigo Donini, Giuliano Donini, Robert Schoenau, Juvides Perini, Claudio Sminosky Jr., Inacio Krug, Paulo Krause, Eduardo F. Da Silva, Marcondes da Silva Candido, Mark Ampah, Frank Pelcat, Lalit Gupta, John Carlo Siewerdt, and Roger Trudel. My special personal gratitude and regards to Carlos Odebrecht, President, Karsten Textile, and Vicente Donini, President, Marisol Group of Industries, for their continued support and overwhelming admiration of my professional work. I am indebted to Vicente Donini for honouring me by commending my book. As always, my sincere thanks to Sylvie Olsen for her impeccable precision and devoted assistance in the preparation of the book. Finally, my love and gratitude goes to my wife, Shashi, and my daughters Pamela and Anuradha, for their continued love, support, and sound judgement.

Nepean-Ottawa, Canada   **Subhash C. Puri**

RETENTION MANAGEMENT

----

*The art of finding and keeping
good people, by providing them
with job satisfaction, fulfilment,
and work-life balance, and
in return gaining their trust,
dedication, loyalty, and long-term
commitment to the organization.*

HUMAN BUSINESS MANAGEMENT
New Discipline for the New Millennium

A Special Note

To successfully handle today's new employment realities, we would like to introduce a new expression, "Human Business (HB) Management", in this book, to replace the commonly used intonation, "Human Resource (HR) Management".

The term "human resource management" is rather restrictive in nature. This expression was quite apt for the Industrial Revolution Era, where the human worker was more or less equated to a mechanical unit - a resource for production. There was no recognition or empathy for the other non-work needs and faculties of the individual.

Times have changed - and changed considerably. Today we are not dealing with the same human resource - we are dealing with a highly skilled, well-informed, and independent individual, who has many diverse sets of needs and aspirations. Today's individual is looking for self-esteem, controls, satisfaction, fulfilment, and work-life balance. Today, the job-related efficiency is not just an isolated non-interdependent entity - it is seriously impacted by other aspects of the individual's life. We cannot carve out some non-overlapping sub-divisions of the individual and expect to explore work-related excellence from only the portion of the individual that goes to work. We must study the subject of motivation and excellence from the collective whole perspective of the individual's total existence.

As such, the new phraseology "Human Business (HB) Management" better serves our purpose - it annotates a broader and more realistic perspective of the subject matter in today's environment.

THE PROLOGUE

1

RETENTION MANAGEMENT: A TOTAL PROFILE

In this opening prologue of the book, and before we begin a detailed exposition of the subject, we shall present an encapsulated summary of the whole issue of human business management, with specific emphasis on the problem of workforce motivation and retention. Starting from the overall profile of the predicaments of business operability, and going down to the specific problem of retention management as a subset, we shall explore how and why this problem occurs and what we can do to resolve it effectively.

BUSINESS SUCCESS: THE ABSOLUTE REALITY

Let us begin our discussion with the most important entity of the business world - the mission of "success". Success is the primary aspiration as well as a necessary requirement of every business organization, small or large, public or private. Personally, I cannot think of any business enterprise who would want to continue their business operability without expecting to achieve success. Success, of course, has different meanings for different organizations. For example, while success for the manufacturing and service organizations in the private sector means profitability and continued growth, it implies fulfilling the mandate in the most effective manner for the public sector.

In any case, for the moment, my aim here is to emphasize the fact that the ultimate purpose behind an organization's mere existence is the desire for success. And the sooner we can accept this fact as the status quo, the easier it would be for us to understand and appreciate the judiciousness and viability of activities and actions that transpire within the operational and organizational framework of the organization.

To accomplish this goal of success, an organization requires, as a minimum, high level capability in three broad areas:

- ▸ Hardware
- ▸ Software
- ▸ Humanware

Hardware includes proper tools and technology; software refers to adequate procedures, processes, and systems - operational, organizational, and customer-oriented; and the humanware involves a highly motivated and committed workforce. Although the hardware and the software are extremely important in their own right, it is the humanware that is the most pre-eminent as well as most intractable of the three. You can have the best technology and the most sophisticated systems and procedures, but unless you have a highly skilled and motivated workforce, you cannot hope to achieve the pinnacles of success. And this is especially true in today's fiercely competitive global market.

HUMAN BUSINESS MANAGEMENT

The core competency of human business management is the problem of human motivation. It is an ancient problem - for the organization - to find suitable people and keep them motivated for higher productivity. Today, this problem has become even more colossal with the addition of another dimension - "excessive job mobility".

With markets becoming global in nature and expanding competitively at a phenomenal rate, the demand for skilled workforce is almost exponentially increasing. At the same time, the nature of personal priorities of individual workers is undergoing dramatic transformations. The combined impact of these two phenomenons is causing serious human business management problems for the organizations at every sectoral level. The overriding concern of today's organizations revolves around the following three questions:

- ▸ How to find good people?
- ▸ Having found them, how to retain them?
- ▸ How to keep employees continuously motivated?

Incidently, we are sticking to the commonly-used intonation - "good people" - by which we mean highly capable, multi-skilled, and self-motivated optimists, with initiative and drive, who would go out of their way to help the organization grow and achieve continued success, and who, by doing so, would also fulfil their own goals and aspirations.

With so many options and opportunities available to the skilled workforce, and the rate of job-mobility reaching crisis proportions, organizations are scrambling to find good people. They are realigning their organizational strategies, work environments, and codes of conduct with relation to the employees, in order to lure employees for longer term commitments.

PROBLEM ANALYSIS

What is "Retention Management"? It means managing to retain people - managing, so that people won't leave the organization - it means short-circuiting the excessive job-hopping in order to achieve a worker's long-term loyalty to the organization.

Naturally then, the most obvious question to ask is, "why do people leave - why do they change jobs". The simplest possible answer to this question is that:

- either they are fired by the organization; or,
- they leave of their own wanting.

Let us consider these two enquiries one by one. Firstly, why and under what circumstances does an organization let a person go? There can be many reasons for terminating a person's employment, some important ones are as follows:

- The organization may be undergoing reorganization, restructuring, or downsizing.
- The organization may find an individual lacking in motivation, and his/her performance and productivity to be below the expected norms of the organization.
- The organization may find the individual unsuitable for the particular job, with regards to the worker's skills and knowledge.
- The organization may find the individual's attitude and behaviour out of line with their culture.
- The organization may find the employee making little contribution towards the accomplishment of the organization's goals.
- The individual's goals may be incompatible with those of the organization.

The aspect of restructuring and downsizing is more of a matter of strategic and logistics importance, and less to do with human business management. We shall not be discussing this aspect of business operability in this book, except for a passing remark that even during downsizing, it is the person with little motivation and poor performance mindset that normally has the highest chance of being fired.

Now let us turn our attention to the second enquiry - "why do people quit their jobs". Once again, for reasons almost parallel to that of the organization, the individual may quit his/her present job to go for another one that may seemingly be the right one, for the following reasons:

- The employee may find the current job deficient in fulfilling his goals and aspirations.
- The employee may be dissatisfied with the job because of one or more of such reasons as: nature of work, working conditions, work environment, renumerations, relationship with management, management and peer support, or the organization's culture.
- The employee may find his goals incompatible with those of the organization.
- The employee may find the nature or level of the job to be a poor fit with his level of expertise.

What can we learn from this problem analysis? In general terms, we can pinpoint the main reasons for the problem to be as follows:

- Employee's lack of motivation
- Goal incompatibility between the individual and the organization
- Goal unfulfillment of both parties

MAPPING THE SOLUTION

By now we should be able to appreciate the fact that the whole process of employment and retention is merely a matter of interplay between two parties - the organization (also commonly referred to as "the management"), and the workers. Or perhaps, it would be more apropos to say that the process is an interaction between two sets of people, one known as the managers, and the other as the workers.

The basic problems in this employee/employer relationship, as identified above, include: employee motivation, employee goal dissatisfaction, and goal incompatibility. All of these problems are completely intertwined - but, they are also typically a normal part of any business organization - there is nothing new or uncanny about them. Why then don't we succeed in resolving these issues? That is where lies the heart of the matter - and that is precisely what we intend to discuss here. Unbelievable as it may sound, our failures are typically due to our own misgivings, deficiencies, idiosyncrasies, and lack of action. It must, however, be clearly understood that my reference to the word "ours" means "us all" collectively, whether we are managers or workers. Both parties have equal responsibility for creating a harmonious working environment in which the delicate employee/employer relationship would flourish forever.

Consider, for example, the issue of workforce motivation. Motivation is a personal thing - it resides inside a person. It is to be self-generated by the individual's own drive, passion, and determination, but it also needs management's help, in terms of providing an impetus, appropriate motivators, and viable reasons.

Motivation is a pretty old issue, and yet our efforts, howsoever honest and serious, have brought us no more than a lukewarm success. I believe that the main reason for our failures is the way we have treated the subject. A subject as sensitive and as human as motivation, we have always tried to resolve it through highly mechanized and regimented systems that don't even address the basic source of motivation - the human psyche.

In this book, we are taking a rather uniquely different approach to motivation enhancement. We are not talking about motivating a person, as if motivation is some kind of external entity that is to be superimposed on a person. Our premise is to build the "person" first - to awaken that highly potent, but hitherto dormant, reservoir of energy from within a person to generate a desire for self-motivation and self-discipline. And this we are doing for the person - whether the person is a manager or worker.

It is my personal unflinching belief that this type of human approach to solving problems and issues is going to become increasingly important in the years to come as technology grows more and more to encompass almost all facets of our life. The more technology and computers are replacing the personal touch, the more employees are craving for it. In fact, the problems of motivation and retention and its proliferation is perhaps because of this decline in personal touch among workers at all levels of the organization. It is this dehumanization of work that is the hidden and unspoken core of all the resentments and dissatisfactions that we are facing today from among the employees. Its resolution is going to be only through the humanization of the workplace.

Let us now move to the next issue: goal satisfaction. For this, the first thing we have to do is to understand what are the goals of today's new workforce. Goal and need hierarchies of individuals propounded by scholars in the past were quite appropriate, but they were apt only for the times they were developed. Today's workforce is certainly not the same as yesterday's. We need to either realign our past theories or develop some fresh paradigms that are in line with the prevailing and impending marketplace requirements and realities.

Once we have formulated this new goal hierarchy of the new workforce, then we have to evaluate its viability. If the goals are excessively lofty, the individual has to be helped and counselled to realign his/her goals to make them more judicious and achievable. If, on the other hand, the goals are reasonable and fair, then we have to invoke management input and responsibility to see that the worker's goals can be fulfilled to the extent possible within the framework of the organization's operability constraints.

Last, but not the least, let us briefly examine the issue of goal compatibility. The seeds of this problem are sown right at the beginning of the employee/employer relationship. This relationship starts from a marriage of convenience - with both parties entering into this matrimony with divergent sets of goals. Let us briefly examine those goals from each party's perspective:

- ▸ The organization enters into the process of hiring with a set of goals - profitability and continued growth. By hiring the individual, the organization expects the individual to come in and perform a designated set of duties and tasks that would ultimately lead to the fulfilment of the organization's goals. It is interesting to note that no organization at this point in time ever hires a person merely to cater to the person's goals only - that entity may come into play at a later date, if at all it does. At this point in time, the organization hires a person with a single-track, self-centred goal - "the organization's welfare". In fact, the organization has more-than-the-goal expectations from the person - it expects that the person should: have good initiative, be self-driven, be multi-skilled, and also be good on soft skills, such as caring attitude, sound judgement, honesty and integrity.
- ▸ Much like the organization, the individual also comes in with his own set of goals, which at this point in time are usually quite divergent from that of the organization. There is no individual that I know of who comes into this entry point of employment by thinking of only achieving the organization's goals of profitability and continued growth. It may happen later in time, of course, if at all it does. At this point, the individual has a set of his/her own goals - something like: security, growth, fulfilment. It should be noted that, unlike the constant never-changing one-track goal of the organization, the individual's goals are generally fluid and multi-dimensional in nature and they change according to the situation an individual is in.

Notwithstanding the details of this paradigm, which we shall elucidate further in the proceeding chapters, the simple conclusion we can draw from this discussion is that the problem of employment and retention typically emanates from the incompatibility of the goals of the two parties. And that, if this goal incompatibility is not rectified over time through mutual understanding, it would naturally create an environment of disharmony, which ultimately would lead to the breakdown of that marriage of convenience, resulting into employee/employer divorce.

In summary, the purpose of the above discussion was simply to provide just a flavour of our thought processes, and to elucidate the frame of mind with which the subject would be expounded. The main focus of the book is on the growth and development of the human person, in order to achieve lasting results, rather than merely on the systems, which only provide temporary solutions. We firmly believe that by strengthening the foundation - the person, whether the person is a worker or manager - we can hope to build a solid structure for the employee/employer relationship.

In line with these thought processes, we shall map out a strategic framework of the subject through the following sequence of steps:

▸ Firstly, we shall endeavour to generate a clear understanding and appreciation of the goals of the organization and of the worker, because goal disparity and incompatibility seems to be the major cause of disharmony at the workplace.

▸ Next, we shall examine the nature and characteristic of changes that are transpiring in the business environment as well as in the personal priorities of the individual, and see how they impact the goals of the organization and the individual.

▸ Since workforce motivation is the glue that binds the individual for long-term commitment to the organization, we shall examine this subject in greater details and identify some fresh thoughts on motivation enhancement.

▸ Then, we shall look into a variety of paradigms for achieving goal compatibility.

▸ Continuing into the realm of softer aspects of human management, and knowing that the entire process of employment and retention is a matter associated with the human person, whether that person is manager or individual worker, we shall expend our efforts towards finding ways and means to augment a person's performance mindset. This would include the following:

• Identifying methods for improving personal personality characteristics for achieving excellence.

• Generating a sense of compassion, empathy, responsibility, and self-discipline in the individual worker to achieve his/her virtual best for himself/herself and for the organization.

• Bringing home the realization for the management, that making employees happy and creating a harmonious work environment is important, requires continuity of action, and ultimately works to the organization's own advantage.

▸ Next, we shall identify a set of tangible actions, strategies, and programs that the organization can undertake to motivate and challenge the employees in order to establish a permanent bond between the workers and the management.
▸ Finally, we shall look at the total picture of business operatability and success from the viewpoint of a joint venture between the worker and the management - as a family unit. For, we believe that when an organization wins, everyone in the organization wins - the management, the workers, the customers, and the stakeholders.

The initiatives and programs suggested throughout the book fall under two categories: tangibles and intangibles. The tangible benefits are those for which the organization has to expend some financial resources in one form or another. These include such initiatives as: salary increase, bonuses, promotions, profit-sharing plans, etc. Although these entities play an important part in workforce motivation and retention, they are difficult to provide continuously over a long period of time for any organization. For that reason, in this book, we are emphasizing the role and value of the intangibles - the softer side of management initiatives, such as: empowerment, praise, recognition, respect, challenge, independence, responsibility, etc. These entities are totally cost-free, and also they are more powerful, because they make an impressionable appeal to the psyche and mental faculties of the individual.

2

PEARLS OF WISDOM

THE SCENARIO - ONE MANAGER'S LAMENTATION:

*"We have read all the books - have attended all kinds of
seminars - have conducted innumerable strategy sessions - we
have met, talked, discussed, and met again - we have planned
- we have developed sophisticated systems,..., in fact, we have
done everything that we could possibly do - and, yet we are
still unable to resolve the problem of workforce motivation -
the problem of how to find good people - how to motivate
them - and how to keep them. The harder we work, the more
behind we get - we find ourselves stagnant on a moving rail."*

Sounds familiar! This is the most typical scenario facing all organizations in this highly volatile and perpetually changing business environment of today.

Personally, I would like to begin the book with a special message - a wake-up call to the realities of business operability. I would like to outline some basic reasons as to why our motivation efforts and systems fail, despite our best intentions and actions. I must warn, however, that my postulates are going to be dreadfully candid and blunt - though they are truly a manifestation of reality out there.

Painful as it may sound, most often we ourselves are the cause of our failures - our own idiosyncrasies and deficiencies, however innocent and unintentional. The way we understand or not understand the realities, our expectations of the systems - our gross inability to take action or the right action - all of these and many more, collectively become instrumental in the demise of our systems.

Based totally on experiential opulence, appended below are some thoughts-provoking revelations and warnings that should be taken seriously, if we have any intention of achieving sustainable levels of success in our endeavours. I would simply urge everyone to clearly understand and comprehend the following axioms before embarking upon to read this book.

REALITIES - REVELATIONS - WARNINGS

1. Our first problem is that we are looking for miracles - a magic formula for instant motivation enhancement. Unfortunately, there are no miracles - no short cuts - no quick fixes. Motivation shall only come through the hard way - through continued dedicated efforts.

2. We cannot achieve results overnight - improvements will only happen slowly, systematically. Patience, determination, and confidence is required.

3. We have to have constancy of purpose and action - we can't undertake motivation improvement initiatives only once and expect to achieve lasting success. We can't expect to jog only for one day and hope to achieve total fitness forever - we have to jog everyday to achieve long-term wellness. A motivation message has a very short memory span - the message fades away very quickly - we need to continuously reinforce the message to realize its full impact.

4. Motivation is not a resultant of one single act, effort, or program - motivation is a multi-faceted entity, and it requires a multi-dimensional activity span. Motivation is a by-product of the collective impact of many initiatives and actions, large and small.

5. Motivation is not a project of limited shelf-life - something to begin and end on a pre-stipulated date, or end when the allocated funds for the project are exhausted. Motivation is an initiative on a continuum - without the finish line. Motivation is an eternal entity.

6. A large majority of the time, our systems fail because of their rigidness and inflexibility vis-a-vis the changing and evolving needs and predicaments of the marketplace as well as of the workforce. To remain viable and effective, systems must have the capability to adapt and be realigned to the changing requirements.

7. Also, we must understand that systems rarely fail because of a single big blunder or catastrophic act - the failure is always a consequence of a collective impact of many mistakes and deficiencies - small and large.

8. Stand alone systems never succeed. All systems must function together, collectively and intergratively - in the operational framework of the organization. And that holds true for the motivation system as well. No system can succeed or survive through its own piecemeal and isolatory existence. Systems are always

interdependent and intertwined - and they must be operated as a collective whole - all reporting to and being accountable to the organization's overall mission.

9. One of the most predominant reason for the failure, especially, of a motivation program, is that we treat the motivation program as a highly regimented mechanical system. Motivation is a human-dependent phenomenon - and for the motivation program to succeed, it must speak the human language. Motivation is a personal thing - it comes from within. So our efforts should not be only directed to the management of program logistics, but they must also be directed to the human consciousness and psyche - to awaken the inner desire and drive from within the individual, to achieve self-discipline and self- motivation.

10. Motivation is a joint venture - it's like a clap - it needs two hands to do it - the management and the worker. Both parties are equally responsible for generating motivation. A word of wisdom for the management: *"you can have a virtual guarantee of retaining your employees and achieving their long-term commitment, if only you can keep motivating and challenging them with the same passion with which you hired them in the first place"*. The problem is that, we forget people's needs and take them for granted - but not our own responsibilities towards them.

11. Last and most importantly, a subject as sensitive and as human as human motivation and retention can only be resolved through human means. You cannot superimpose some highly sophisticated and technologically advanced, but inert and non-human, systems on the human person and expect to enhance his sense of motivation and self-discipline.

The accelerated rate of growth of our technological sector has so intensely hypnotized us and captivated out attention span, that we are becoming oblivious even to the inherent creator of that technology - the human person. Our workplace is becoming increasingly dehumanized, and the more it is happening, the more workers are craving for the "human touch" - which is the core competency of workforce motivation and retention. The human touch is declining as fast as the technology is advancing. The humanware, which is the key ingredient and the wealth of the organization, is getting overshadowed by this colossal mass of hardware and software. The predator is becoming its own prey - the creators of processes, procedures, and systems are themselves becoming an entity.

There is another spin-off of our techno-thinking - we are becoming too much system-oriented. To some extent, it is good, because our operability has become more precise, efficient, and standardized. But, at the same time, it has made us redundantly robotic. We let our systems dictate to us, rather than us driving and controlling the systems. Consequently, we are generally more preoccupied with managing the system logistics, rather than caring for the people for whom the system was developed in the first place. And surprisingly, we do that even for the motivation systems that are supposed to be totally human-dependent. This is what I call "unintentional misappropriation of technology".

It is, therefore no surprise that we are witnessing unprecedented human business management problems, such as: job dissatisfaction, job mobility, lack of motivation and long-term loyalty and commitment. And this is because the main ingredient in the equation - the human touch - is on the decline. And unfortunately, if we don't wake up to this reality, we will be facing even greater volatility in the human management aspects of our business in the coming years.

Incidently, it is neither technology nor systems to blame - it is our own misdirected focus that is the culprit. Influencing and enhancing attitude, which is the core competency of motivation, through mechanized and regimented systems is much like standardizing morality. For motivation enhancement, we need to create a sense of harmony and balance between the technoware and the humanware. To motivate the person and gain his trust and loyalty, we have to focus on the person - to appeal to his psyche - to make inner awakenings - to induce a drive for self-motivation, self-discipline, and a passion for excellence. Only those organizations will be successful in the impending millennium, who would be able to recognize this incongruency and endeavour to generate a balanced work environment - because they will be the ones who will be able to get and retain the brightest and the best.

THE FINAL WARNING

Just in case you choose to brush aside the above axioms as mere trivialities, then most likely:

- ► You would read this book like any other similar book that you have read before, and put it on the shelf along with other books, to collect dust. And, your search will begin all over again for another book that may provide you with a miracle recipe. Sorry to disappoint you - but you won't find that magic formula anywhere. Miracles don't just happen - they are created by people.
- ► You would be taking additional courses and seminars, and conducting more strategic sessions - and this exercise will continue unabated.
- ► Sadly enough, you may still be without answers.

PART 1

THE
UNDERSTANDING

3

THE PARADIGM
OF BUSINESS SUCCESS

BUSINESS SUCCESS: A REALITY CHECK

As indicated earlier, success is the most fundamental and intrinsic goal of every enterprise. It is the driving force behind all business decisions. In fact, it is the sole purpose behind an organization's existence. The success-oriented mission and goals of the organization are really the dominant elements that shape the organization's strategic plans and its ensuing financial, technological, and human resource requirements. Simply put, every aspect of business operability is geared to and impacted by this mandatory passion for success. This is one blatant reality that we must clearly understand and accept as a precursor to understanding any other business management aspect. For, if there is no success, there is no business.

BUSINESS PRIORITIES

Most organizations maintain three sets of goals:

- ► Priority/Goal #1:   For the organization: Profitability and continued growth
- ► Priority/Goal #2:   For the workforce: Welfare of employee
- ► Priority/Goal #3:   For the society: Service to society

Let us, for a moment, analyse these priorities realistically and understand what they mean.

Priority/Goal #1: Organization Success

For the manufacturing and service sectors, success simply means "making money" - period. We can deny it, be modest about it, or outright disagree or reject it - but that is the naked reality. The ownership and existence of the entire infrastructure of the organization - hardware, software, humanware - is there because of and due to this singularly predominant goal of profitability.

Acquiring better technology, finding more markets, improving the quality of products and services, looking after the welfare of the employees, making customers happy - everything is important and meaningful - but "only" as long as the company is making money. If not, then all of these entities get affected in one form or another in accordance with the extent of the company's financial health and performance.

It is also important to note that this is one goal that never changes - it remains eternally constant as long as the company exists.

Priority/Goal #2: Worker Happiness

Immediately after their own goal of profitability, comes in the second important priority for the organization - "welfare of the employees". This goal is intricately intertwined with goal #1, but it has some interesting characteristics that are worth examining:

- ▸ Although this goal is presumably meant for the employees, if we examine it more closely and rather selfishly, we will realize that it is in fact a subset of the organization's own primary goal. Because, when an organization strives to make employees happy, they intuitively know that a happy worker means a more productive and dedicated worker - all of which ultimately leads to better realization of the organization's own primary goal.
- ▸ Logistically, this goal is placed at a second priority level, but it really is so closely intertwined with the primary goal that it becomes undifferentiable from it. For, if the workforce is not motivated and productive, the realization of goal #1 is virtually impossible. Successful organizations are cognizant of this reality, and they consider goal #2 as an integral part of goal #1.

Priority/Goal #3: Service to Society

In much the same way as before, this tertiary goal of the organization - service to society - is a goal that ultimately meets the company's own ends. For, by improving its image as a good service provider to society, the organization sets the stage for achieving greater market credibility and hence, better acceptability - all, intuitively, leading to the realization of the organization's primary goal, in one form or another.

If we can first boldly accept this personification of success as the status quo, then I would indeed like to expand this goal of society's welfare a bit further. While it is perfectly normal and reasonable for every enterprise, at every sectoral level, to aim for their own profitability and success, we must all be seriously cognizant of a much bigger role that we must play - to aim for society's welfare. We must all collectively undertake the responsibility for the welfare and enhancement of the society that provides us the platform for that success. Society and businesses are intricately intertwined - one cannot succeed without the other. History is our witness - a country's affluence and progress goes hand in hand with its business growth and success. The whole scenario calls for a collective will and dedication at all three levels - personal, organizational, and societal - to realize collective success.

This premise, at least, makes it easy for us to expound on the importance of the success-motivation-human business management connection. The pursuit of excellence and success permeates at the three levels: personal, organizational, and societal. All three levels are mutually interdependent, and they are bound through a single common nucleus - the human person.

At the individual level, each person has an innate desire to achieve excellence. This desire induces self-discipline and motivation in the person, which when projected onto the organizational and societal levels, ultimately becomes instrumental in achieving business excellence and societal welfare. Thus, we can easily see that the entire activity framework hinges on human potential. Nothing can be conceived, realized, or accomplished without dedicated human endeavour. And dedication is generated by inner desire - which in turn, is generated by motivation. This is how important the enigma of motivation and human business management is - a simple, but powerful enigma that we are going to address in this book. This is also where the efforts and ingenuity of the management comes into play - to motivate and challenge the employees on a continuous basis, so that they have no reason to leave. In the same token, however, it is also a "call-to-arms" to the workforce, at every level in the organization, to rise up to the occasion, clearly understand the goals of the organization, be accountable to the organization's workplans, and join hands with the management to achieve mutually rewarding levels of goal fulfilment.

MEANING/DETERMINANTS OF SUCCESS

MANUFACTURING SECTOR

Continuing with the paradigm of success, we can now restate the goals of each sector separately. Starting with the manufacturing sector, and speaking as candidly as we did before, the hierarchy of goals of the manufacturing organizations can be expressed as follows:

- ▸ Goal #1: Making Money
- ▸ Goal #2: Making More Money
- ▸ Goal #3: Making More Money Continuously

Now rephrasing these into a simpler and more professional language, the three goals respectively mean:

- ▸ Making Money ➡ Productivity: *Producing more with less - enhancing productivity and quality of products and services*
- ▸ Making More Money ➡ Growth: *Expanding market share through greater customer satisfaction*
- ▸ Making More Money Continuously ➡ Credibility: *Enhancing organization's image to achieve continued market patronage*

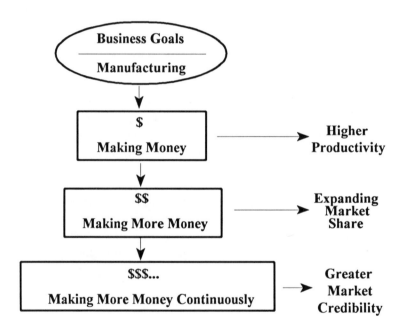

In searching for the core competencies of success, it is not too hard to conceptualize that success would belong to those organizations, in the new millennium, who have, as a minimum, the following fundamental attributes:

BUSINESS SUCCESS: TEN COMMANDMENTS

1. Global competitive mindset
2. State-of-the-art technology
3. Knowledge-based workforce
4. Simplified integrated systems
5. Aggressive marketing
6. Ability to adapt to changing business environment
7. High level human business management capability
8. Excellence in quality and productivity
9. Competitive products and services
10. Customer satisfaction

Abbreviating these success characteristics further, the most simple recipe for success is:

- Producing more
- More cheaply
- Consistently better

Producing More:

- More volume and variety
- Better designs
- Technologically superior products
- Innovative products

More Cheaply:

- Higher productivity
- Competitive prices

Consistently Better:

- Quality constancy and excellence
- Customer satisfaction

This revelation takes us back to the same realism that we started with - that the driving force behind all determinants of success is the human endeavour, dedication, and excellence - generated through self-motivation and self-discipline - and reenforced through effective human business management. This assertion can be easily validated and appreciated by the following chain reaction:

> Enhanced Motivation ➜ Higher Productivity ➜ Improved Quality
> ➜ Reduced Costs ➜ Competitive Prices ➜ Customer Satisfaction
> ➜ Improved Marketability ➜ Competitive Success

SERVICE SECTOR

Although the operational framework of the service organizations may be somewhat different from that of the manufacturing organizations, their goals and priorities are, more or less, similar and parallel, as schematically presented below:

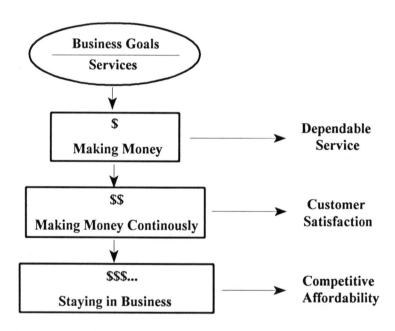

The service sector is one area that is almost totally human-dependent, and involves extensive interplay of human element. Some of the unique and special people-oriented characteristics of services are:

- ▸ Services are personalized
- ▸ Services involve the customer directly
- ▸ Services are produced on demand with the customer interplay
- ▸ Services are intangible
- ▸ Services are perishable; they cannot be stored or stacked
- ▸ Services cannot be shown or exhibited prior to delivery
- ▸ Services cannot be inspected or tested
- ▸ Services are labour-intensive; they may involve complex cross-functional integration of several support systems

It is because of this heavy human involvement and concentration that the service sector requires an even stronger emphasis on employee motivation and human business management. The one aspect that clearly deserves special attention in a service operation is the role of the customer. A customer is the most important person in a service business. In fact, service business is totally customer-dependent. Therefore, every process, procedure or initiative that is put into place for improving service quality must viably address and accommodate the customer's needs and expectations.

In a sense we are all customers. When we walk into an organization to receive a service, we have a set of expectations about the service delivery mode. As schematically appended below, the first thing we look for is responsiveness, courtesy, and helpfulness. Then we look for competency, efficiency, and dependability of service. Lastly, we expect the service to be of high quality, competitively affordable, and satisfying.

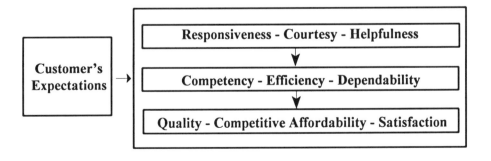

Finally, we shall discuss the most fundamental success determinant for any service business - the "front desk" - the persons at the front end who comes into contact with the customer for the actual delivery of the service. We all know that customers do not buy from the CEO, the manager, or the owner of the company. They buy and are serviced by individuals who do the work: salespersons, repair persons, telephone operators, bank tellers, airline officers, waiters, etc. These are the people who impact the quality of the service rendered. It is, therefore, of the utmost importance to ensure that those persons are highly motivated and service-oriented. In this regard, we have two very simple rules that every organization must follow:

- ▸ Select personnel on the basis of their ability and willingness to deal with people. Motivate them. Give them your best, but expect the best also - something that we annotate as: "zero tolerance management" - and shall be expounded in a later chapter of the book. Make sure that you put zero tolerance on "attitude problems". There is no room, at the front end of the service delivery function, for a person with an attitude problem.
- ▸ Continuously measure the efficiency and performance of the service delivery function. Ideally, every once in a while you should yourself try to become a customer for your own service delivery and evaluate the quality of your service.

GOVERNMENT SECTOR

The public sector has its own distinctly unique set of priorities and predicaments. There are increasing demands on the public sector to improve its efficiency and quality of services. The continued health of an agency depends directly on its credibility - which, indeed, depends on the taxpayer's perception, to whom the agency is accountable. The executive leaders in the public sector face an enormously difficult challenge. They have to improve quality and productivity with shrinking resources while accommodating a host of conflicting needs, requirements, and expectations. As a minimum, they have to do the following to evolve an effective quality improvement infrastructure:

- ▸ Balance conflicting and changing political priorities
- ▸ Balance conflicting taxpayer's expectations and requirements
- ▸ Balance changing domestic and international markets
- ▸ Balance international priorities and pressures

Success in the public sector, typically, amounts to:

- ▸ Improved internal operational efficiency
- ▸ Higher productivity

- Optimal utilization of resources
- Cost-effective operability
- Quality excellence of service-delivery function
- Proactive responsiveness to the public
- Effective fulfilment of the mandate
- Achievement of public confidence

The public sector operability is much like that of the service sector - almost totally dependent on the effectiveness of the humanware - the people. It requires continuous high level interventions for enhancing workforce motivation and productivity.

COMPETITIVE SUCCESS - A PARADIGM SHIFT

In line with the signification of success as appended above, we shall now like to identify another interesting phenomenon - an intriguingly new dimension that has been added onto the meaning of success. With the globalization of the marketplace and increasing competitiveness, the connotation of success has been eulogized from "success" to "competitive success". Today, organizations are not looking at their own success in isolatory terms, but they are measuring their own success in relation to the success of their competitors.

To elucidate this new phraseology, let us look at "success" as we know it today. We know that the most critical determining factors for success include, as a minimum, the following:

- Technological superiority
- Productive workforce
- Quality excellence
- Competitive pricing
- Customer satisfaction

The question is: if every enterprise can meet these requirements, then how does one organization achieve greater competitive success than the others? So we are asking - what does an organization have to do over and above the ordinary, to be competitively more successful?

Typically, competitive success means:

- That, you are better than most of your competitors.
- That, you have a bigger share of the market.
- That, your market credibility is higher than your competitors.
- That, your profits are proportionately higher than your competitors.

- That, you are a stable company.
- That, your's is among the best-run companies in the marketplace.
- That, people feel proud to be working for you.
- That, your customers rate you as the most dependable company.

Succinctly speaking, the following narrative should provide a better grasp of the difference between "success" and "competitive success":

To be successful, you have to:

- know your market share
- know your customer's demands and expectations
- know your market niches
- know your own strengths, capabilities, and weaknesses
- know your potential customers and their demands

To be competitively successful, in addition to the above, you must:

- know your competitor's market share
- know your competitor's niches
- know your competitor's strengths and weaknesses
- know in which way your competitor is better than you
- Know how to strategize to gain competitive advantage

Let me elucidate this paradigm shift in the business mentality, by citing a real life example from the service sector. A friend of mine owns a fairly large restaurant and the business is good. Yet, he constantly complains about a competitor's restaurant down the road which is running better than his. His perpetual obsession is - why can't I do better than him - how can I beat my competition?

While this is just a simple illustration, it still provides a subtle insight into how changes are transpiring in our attitudes and thought processes - how businesses are reshaping their strategies and procedures to achieve "competitive success".

For the sake of interest, let me go further and also present here the framework of my recommendations that I propounded to my friend in answer to his question: "How can I beat the competition?". The formula that I am outlining is rather naively simple, but it is pretty efficacious and workable.

BEATING THE COMPETITION: A FOUR-STEP FORMULA

- Step 1: Know how your competitor operates
- Step 2: Know why your competitor's customers are happy

> ▸ Step 3: Imitate your competitor
> ▸ Step 4: Find a niche

Before I expand further on my formula, let me elucidate the basic premise of a restaurant. Why do we go to a restaurant? Good quality food at reasonable prices, and good service. If we get good food, but lousy service - most likely we would pick up the food and bring it home to eat. If we get good service, but the food is not good - we appreciate the service but we may not come back again. If we get good food as well as good service - not only will we go there over and over again - we will also recommend the restaurant to all of our friends. And now let me expand on my simple recipe for competitive success on a more generalized level:

Step 1: Know how your competitor operates

> ▸ What kind of systems do they have?
> ▸ Do they have a good quality management system?
> ▸ How do they control their processes?
> ▸ How do they improve their productivity and efficiency?
> ▸ How do they motivate their workforce?
> ▸ What are their marketing strategies?
> ▸ What are their strategies for customer satisfaction?

Step 2: Know why your competitor's customers are happy

> ▸ What are their customers' perception about their quality of products and services?
> ▸ What kind of treatment do their customers get from them?
> ▸ What are some of the basic reasons of their customers' satisfaction?

Step 3: Imitate your competitor

> ▸ Just imitate and do what you have learned about your competitor from step 1 and 2 above.
> ▸ This would bring you at par with your competitor.

Step 4: Find a niche

> ▸ Now, find how you can do better than your competitor.
> ▸ Don't only copy - find a niche to surpass your competitor.
> ▸ Innovate - enhance your operations.

Translating that to the restaurant situation, my advice to my friend was that either he should go himself or send someone to his competitor's restaurant to undertake what I call "healthy spying" to find out the following:

- ▸ Aspects relating to operability: type of food served, menu selection, food quality, prices, service quality, restaurant's ambience and decor, etc.
- ▸ Aspects relating to customer satisfaction: find out, by talking to customers, the reasons for their satisfaction.

The next step for my friend involves doing what his competitor does. Once that is in place, then he has to think how to do better than the competitor, in any aspect possible.

The above narrative may seem overly simplistic, but it has powerful applications in real-life situations. We shall now close our discussion on the success paradigm of the business world by reiterating that success and profitability is almost the end-all goal of every enterprise, and that the most important ingredients of success are worker motivation, efficiency, and dedication.

4

BUSINESS ENVIRONMENT: TODAY → TOMORROW

INTRODUCTION

We all know how rapidly and dramatically changes are transpiring in every aspect of our lives, and how we are making perpetual readjustments and adaptations to cope with these changes. Changes in the external business environment, internal work environment, or in personal priorities, all collectively bear enormous impact on the goals, day-to-day priorities, and operational framework of the business world. The adaptive realignments that the organizations have to undertake as a consequence of these changes, in turn, exert extensive influence on the workforce. People and their motivational thresholds are profoundly affected by the prevailing work environment within the organization as well as by the demands and pressures of the marketplace. Therefore, in order to develop suitable motivational enhancement strategies and an effective human business management framework, it is essential to understand the changes that are transpiring in the business world. As a minimum, we shall outline the following:

- ▸ changes in the work environment
- ▸ changing priorities of the workforce
- ▸ public sector challenges
- ▸ changing customer demands
- ▸ global competitive pressures
- ▸ changes in the human business management framework

CHANGING FACE OF BUSINESS ENVIRONMENT

Today's business environment...restructuring, re-engineering, downsizing, corporate mergers and take-overs, bankruptcies, cost recovery, deregulation, privatization, decentralization, out-sourcing..., there is undoubtedly an uneasy volatility in the marketplace. Whether it is the manufacturing sector, service sector, or government agencies, there is a perpetual sense of turmoil and instability.

Is this reality a manifestation of chaos or is it a normal part of business life? Is this phenomenon short-lived or are we going to be experiencing similar operating circumstances in the next century?

First, the bad news - unfortunately, the scenario is atypical of a highly competitive and constantly changing business environment, and in all probability, we can expect to see these constraints and pressures to stay with us for a long time. We are going to be experiencing perhaps even more pronounced changes and intense competitive pressures in the next millennium.

The good news is that changes are generally for the better - they provide challenge and greater opportunity for growth and development. Changes are essential to avoid stagnation and redundancy.

Since there is hardly any escape from changes, it is better for our strategic health to accept this reality as the status quo and, therefore, try to proactively expend our energies and resources in developing functional strategies, systems, products, and culture that can constantly evolve, change, and adapt to the shocks and forces of time. To succeed, we have to persistently disturb the present - something that we like to annotate as "concurrent re-engineering" - challenging our policies, procedures, and products on a continuous basis. The paradigms of the quiet past are not going to work in the turbulent future. With new demands, we shall have to constantly think and act anew.

Let us briefly look at the changes and predicaments that organizations are facing around the world:

- ▸ Companies have to do more and more with less and less to stay afloat
- ▸ Companies are entangled in the web of conflicting paradigms:
  - Balancing their own desire for greater controls against worker's demands for greater autonomy and freedom
  - Balancing their own goals against those of the workers
  - Balancing their own priorities and time constraints against worker's desire for work-life balance
  - Balancing their own needs for better skilled workforce against excessive job mobility
  - Balancing their own culture that determines what behaviour is acceptable for its members, against individual's own value system - as big, deep, and powerful - within which they want to operate.

- ‣ The face of work environment is changing in many a ways:
  - Workplace is becoming more democratized.
  - Ownership of processes is moving into the hands of the workers.
  - The old ways of commanding, controlling, and managing is being replaced by greater independence, self-management, accountability, and participatory operability.
  - The nature of the work is becoming more computerized, automatic, and process/procedure oriented.
  - Personal contact is being replaced by networking, e-mails, and teleconferencing.
  - Workers are becoming more knowledge-based and well-informed.
  - Workers are becoming multi-skilled, self-sufficient, and independent.
  - Workers are becoming more conscious about their work-life balance. Ideally, they are looking for having a good job, making good money, be independent, and live out their dreams - all at the same time.
  - Workers' priorities are changing - they value meaningful work, better controls, satisfaction, fulfilment, and a balanced life.
  - The norm of the day is: mobility, flexibility, accountability, self-discipline, willingness to embrace change, broad-based knowledge and skills.
- ‣ The customer demands are also changing in many a ways:
  - Customers are more knowledgeable and better informed.
  - Customers have greater demand for quality.
  - Customers expects higher quality products and services at the lowest possible competitive prices - the best of both worlds.
  - Customers are now driving the markets - rather than marketing people driving the customers, as was the case in the past.

COMPETITIVE PRESSURES

Let us now peep into the global world and examine how competitive pressures are affecting the organization. With the globalization of the marketplace, competitiveness is reaching crisis proportions and it is exerting pressures of unbearable degree on the companies. Companies are running amuck trying to manage in a rush - developing and inventing new systems and strategies on a daily basis to cope with the competition - resorting to all kinds of frenzied actions like: restructuring, out-sourcing, downsizing, mergers, etc., just to keep afloat - all with good intentions of course, but all without the benefit of any serious historical experiential precedence and assistance.

Competition is generally looked at from the angle of production levels, pricing, and overall company revenue and profitability. And all of these entities exert tremendous influence on the strategic and operational framework of the organization. The ensuing changes or realignments that an organization has to undertake, are generally for very compelling and valid reasons, but they still end up creating a sense of instability of one sort or another in the organization. The impact of this disequilibrium, whether short-lived or continuing, permeates down to the working levels and you can easily feel the workforce exhibiting a sense of fear and apprehension. This makes it even more important for the organization to have high level of human business management capability in order to diffuse the uncanny situation and make the change phenomenon work for the betterment.

Let us just consider, as an example, the paradigm of competitive pressures between the developed and developing economies, to get a perspective of how competition is reshaping the business strategies.

The developing countries have the advantage of being labour-intensive as well as having the availability of cheaper labour force. They are capable of producing pro-ducts with greater volume and variety, at cheaper costs - and that too, in some cases, with obsolete or borrowed technology. Their products, at times however, lack in quality. Still, there is no denying the fact that these countries can flood the markets with cheaper goods, creating a competitive nightmare for the developed countries.

Despite this advantage, however, the developing countries are facing another serious challenge. In the past, the developing countries were, more or less, occupied with the domestic markets only. Operating among peers with similar operational demands and quality requirements was not too difficult. Now, the developing countries are competing in an open global market. Exporting products and services to highly developed economies has generated enormous operability and quality pressures. In the highly developed markets, business operability revolves around five basic rules of business: good quality, on-time delivery, quality constancy, competitive pricing, and customer satisfaction. Many of these conditions and expectations are untenable for developing countries. Consequently, they are scrambling hard to improve their production and operational efficiency as quickly as possible. But those attributes are a by-product of a highly motivated and efficient workforce - something that is seriously lacking in many developing countries. As a natural consequence of this, one can easily notice a heightened state of activity around enhancement of quality-motivation culture in the developing countries.

Let us now examine the plight of the developed economies in this highly competitive global scenario. The developed countries are also, indeed, capable of producing greater volume, variety, and at the same time higher quality goods, but only against much higher production costs. Consequently, the competitive pricing pressures are greater and the companies have to undertake aggressive marketing campaigns to justify higher prices vis-a-vis better quality. To balance out those pressures, many companies in the developed economies are being forced to resort to drastic measures, such as: restructuring, downsizing, out-sourcing, and/or moving their production facilities to labour-intensive countries.

Let us look at another business dilemma relating to product pricing and profitability. A product goes through several hands of buyers, purchasers, customers, and sellers from the time it leaves the hands of the manufacturers to the time it is sold to the ultimate consumer or user. Because each of the intermediatory entity wishes to make a reasonable profit, there is generally a very significant price differential between the producer's selling price and the ultimate seller's selling price. And since the ultimate seller has to sell at competitively low prices as well as make profits, the goods have to start at a very low price from the manufacturers. This puts enormous profitability margin pressures on the producers. Consequently, the producers are always striving to improve efficiency and productivity.

We have only presented just a sample of some of the challenges that the business world is likely to be facing in the years ahead. Whether it is the manufacturing sector, service sector, or government sector, the predicaments may be different, but the basic common need is the same - the need to improve worker efficiency and achieve success. The discussion here was intended just to provide a perspective of what organizations may have to do differently or better than what they have been doing before, in terms of system management and human resource management, in order to achieve competitive success in the next century.

PUBLIC SECTOR CHALLENGES

Some of the major challenges that governments, at all levels and in all countries, are facing, include the following:

- ▸ Reducing the deficit and lowering expenditures
- ▸ Helping business to grow by reducing stringency of rules and regulations
- ▸ Helping business to improve export markets
- ▸ Reducing unemployment
- ▸ Improving efficiency of service delivery function and internal operability
- ▸ Accepting greater responsibility and accountability
- ▸ Creating economic and business stability
- ▸ Enhancing public image and confidence

Once again we can see that all these attributes of success point to the same need - the need to improve the efficiency of systems, which indeed, depends on the dedication and excellence of the people.

CHANGING FACE OF HUMAN BUSINESS MANAGEMENT

As we can see from the above discussion, the rules of the workplace have almost been totally rewritten. The fat, happy, permanent job security has been replaced by mobility, flexibility, accountability, and tangible evidence of hard work.

New economic age, new realities, new challenges - we need to put a new face on our old ways of doing things. The scenario calls for a whole new way of thinking, behaving, and acting when it comes to human business management. The old theories of motivation are not going to work any more. They are not sufficiently equipped to cater to the realities of the new business environment. The democratized workplace of the future would require some new and innovative democratized models of motivation. As we can see, for example, a large majority of our old paradigms about people management have, hitherto, persistently asserted that it is the management who alone bears the sole responsibility for motivating people. While, we do not wish to entirely refute the old theories, we would like to consider a complete paradigm shift - a paradigm in which the emphasis on the individual workers is also as strong, to achieve their personal best and personal excellence through self-motivation generated by inner personal dedication.

Consider another example of a paradigm shift from the old way of thinking. In the past, our motivational efforts were generally directed at the whole workforce collectively as one unit. The emphasis was on the program as a whole for the whole. As such, the monitoring of individual performance was also a group exercise. Today, the emphasis is highly democratized and personalized. Each person has to be individually accountable for his/her performance. This, however, also creates enormous monitoring problems. How can management have the time and resources to monitor the work habits of each individual separately? An individual may, for example, be sitting and gazing over a set of documents or a task at his desk, or be sitting in front of his computer and looking like he is working very hard, when in fact he may really be wasting time, or cruising the Internet, or playing computer games. So we can see that we need a new paradigm of motivation - a paradigm in which the emphasis shifts from the whole program or group to the individual self-monitoring and self-discipline - where the onus is as much on the individual to inculcate self-motivation as on the management to induce this sense of accountability and performance monitoring.

5

CHANGING PERSONAL PRIORITIES

CHANGING FACE OF THE WORKPLACE

As indicated earlier, the problem of excessive job-mobility and retention emanates from goal-unfulfilment and goal incompatibility. In chapter 1, we outlined the mainframe of the organization's goals and priorities.

Now, in this chapter, we shall build the need hierarchy of the individual vis-a-vis the changing personal and occupational priorities. A detailed analysis of this goal-hierarchy of today's workforce would help us to better understand what we have to do to fulfil these goals and how can we make serious interventions to short-circuit the excessive job-mobility.

To begin with, we must all agree that times are changing - and changing fast -and with it, our own personal priorities and occupational expectations are changing. Our social structure and interaction - our beliefs and values - our goals and desires - all of these are evolving and perpetually changing over time. And as intelligently as possible, we are continuously making realignments and adaptations. Hundreds of examples can be cited to substantiate the fact that changes are encompassing and transforming our lives in many a ways - instead, we would just identify a ridiculously simple analogy to make our point. Look at yourself and see if you are doing the same things as your parents did or as your children are doing - the way you think, behave, and act. Most probably not.

Notwithstanding however, this phenomenon of perpetual change and volatility at least provides us with our first important lesson - that our human business management models and practices must also be constantly revised and updated vis-a-vis the changes of the time, so that they are appropriate and effective for the time period at hand. For if we don't do that, our own inadaptability will haunt us in one form or another. And that is precisely what's happening today. The basic reason for the failure of many of our programs and systems stems from one or more of the following idiosyncrasies:

- ▸ Use of inappropriate and outdated models and procedures
- ▸ Inability to adapt to the changing needs and pressures
- ▸ Lack of impetus to take action

What are some of those changes that have transpired in our thought processes, our beliefs, our values, and our goals and expectations? We have already identified a few aspects in the preceding chapters. Let us recapitulate and elucidate them further, as follows:

PERSONAL-ORIENTED ASPECTS

- ▸ Workers are increasingly becoming more knowledge-based, and have multi-dimensional capability levels.
- ▸ Workers are more well-informed today than before.
- ▸ Workers value democratic and transparent operability framework, open communications, and greater freedom of choice.
- ▸ Workers like greater control over the processes for which they are responsible.
- ▸ Workers are not merely a mechanical resource for production, as was conceived during the industrial revolution era, they are more human with humanly aspirations.
- ▸ Workers are more independent and self-sufficient.
- ▸ Money is an important requirement, but today's worker values controls, satisfaction, fulfilment, and meaningful work as more important than money. If the baby boomers were looking for a high-powered and excruciatingly engaging working milieu, today's worker is looking for a fulfillingly balanced work-life on which he has full control.
- ▸ Workers have greater consciousness towards total wellness and work-life balance. They do not perceive work as any more or any less important than other out-of-work aspects of their lives. Balancing their personal and occupational lives is almost their primary priority.

WORK-ORIENTED ASPECTS

- ▸ The workplace is operating under greater competitive pressures, and consequently there is a perpetual state of readjustments of priorities and strategies.
- ▸ The workplace is getting more and more technologically oriented, and it

requires workers to have greater broad-based knowledge and skills.

▸ The workplace is becoming more democratized - participatory management, teamwork, and empowerment are in vogue.

▸ The norm of the day is: flexibility, adaptability to change, self-driven motivation.

▸ Fat, happy, permanent job security is being replaced by mobility, and accountability - there is no more guaranteed lifetime employment without tangible evidence of excellence in performance. You can do a great job and have a high rating on your annual performance sheet on Monday, and still get the pink slip on Wednesday. The lean and mean workplace of today requires you to be a self-motivator, a self-disciplined and adaptable person.

On the basis of this brief characterization of the changing nature of personal priorities, we shall now build a new paradigm of need-hierarchy of today's workforce. But to build such a model that would reflect the realities of the evolving marketplace, we also need to examine some of the past theories of motivation, so that we can gain some knowledge from a comparative evaluation of the past and present, and appropriately utilize that to build the new model.

MOTIVATION THEORIES

A number of excellent theories have been propounded in the past by a variety of scholars and professionals, such as: Taylor, Maslow, McGregor, Hergberg, and Ouchi. Most of these theories approached the subject of motivation by examining the needs of the individual and identifying what motivates a person. The focus of their attention was not retention management, but productivity improvement. These theories made significant contributions to our understanding of the subject of motivation for the time period they were propounded. The idea to present their main features here is to see if we can gain some extra knowledge to build our new need-hierarchy model for today's workforce. Ideally, we wish to develop a model that would, as a minimum, have the following attributes:

▸ It would provide the best fit for the needs and realities of the time.
▸ It would be flexible, adaptable, and applicable to as many situations as possible.

Despite what we want or what we can develop, we must recognize the limitations of any model - that no single theory, model, or system can single-handedly provide answers to all types of situations, for all times to come. Although, we all have the same basic needs, we are all motivated by different things. The best we can hope for is to have a model that would be reasonably adequate, globally acceptable, and conducive to realignments vis-a-vis the changing needs and priorities of the time. With this premise, we shall now present a very brief description of a few of the important theories.

Abraham Maslow

Maslow, a psychologist by profession, propounded his theory of "need-hierarchy" in which he identified five sets of individual needs, whose fulfilment bears a profound influence on the motivation threshold of the individual. Those needs are:

- Physiological needs
- Safety and security
- Social fulfilment
- Self-esteem and recognition
- Self-actualization and personal development

Critique on Maslow

- The needs identified by Maslow, as well as their sequence does not appropriately fit the needs of today's workforce.
- The theory fails to recognize individual differences.
- The theory is more static than dynamic or flexible.
- The theory does not provide any clear cut set of directions on how to generate workforce motivation.

Douglas McGregor

In line with and heavily drawing upon Maslow's hierarchy of needs, McGregor developed his concept of workforce motivation in the context of the nature and type of organizations and their motivational emphasis and thrust. He propounded two theories, theory X and theory Y, as follows:

Theory X

McGregor identified X-organizations as the ones that maintain a hierarchical infrastructure which tends to exercise complete control over the behaviour of employees. He characterizes the workforce in X-organizations as follows:

- Workers are inherently lazy and will avoid work, if they can.
- Workers must be continuously controlled, directed, and forced to perform well.
- Workers have very little ambition and they would avoid accepting responsibility whenever they can.

Theory Y

Theory Y is almost tangibly different from theory X. It believes that people are anxious to accept greater responsibility and exercise self-control and self-direction. It encourages organizations to generate an integrated work environment that is conducive to achieving a high degree of performance and success. The main features of this theory can be stated as follows:

- Workers enjoy physical and mental efforts.
- Workers prefer to exercise self-control and self-direction.
- Workers associate their achievement with rewards.
- Workers are willing to accept greater responsibility.
- Workers have the capacity for imagination, creativity, and ingenuity.
- The intellectual potential of workers is only partially utilized under modern industrial life conditions.

Critique on MacGregor

- Theory X organizations are virtually non-existent in today's business environment.
- Theory Y has many good points, which are applicable even in today's work environment. But overall, it still lacks an integrated approach to resolving the motivation or retention dilemma.
- Neither Maslow's theory, nor McGregor's Theory Y approaches the subject through the angle of an individual's growth, development, and personality enhancement, i.e., appealing and strengthening the human consciousness aspects to generate self-discipline.

Frederick Hergberg

The highlights of Hergberg's contribution to the subject of motivation include identification of job-satisfaction (motivators) and job-dissatisfaction (demotivators) factors, as follows:

Motivators

The fulfilment of these factors bring about workforce motivation and job satisfaction:

- *Achievement*: Relates to successful completion of a job; achievement of expected goals; workability of a new idea, new design, new procedure.
- *Recognition*: Recognition among peers and management; recognition of a job well done; praise; respect; reward.

- *Growth and Development*: Opportunities for professional growth; independence and empowerment; freedom to create and innovate.
- *Advancement*: Opportunities for further advancement to higher managerial positions; salary increases; promotion; greater responsibility.
- *Responsibility*: Recognition of capabilities by the management; giving of greater responsibility; ownership of processes; opportunity for decision-making.
- *Nature and Type of Job*: The nature of job and its challenges; meaningful work; job variety; job flexibility and control.

Demotivators

Dissatisfaction with the following entities creates a sense of demotivation and unhappiness among workers:

- *Organization culture*: policies and practices; values; beliefs; codes of conduct
- *Management style*: Autocratic; democratic; participatory; delegation and empowerment style
- *Support Systems*: Management support; relationship with peers and managers
- *Job Security*: Stability; fear-free operability
- *Money*: Salary; financial packages; profit-sharing plans; employee assistance
- *Working conditions*: Facilities, work environment; working conditions; environmental conditions
- *Work-life balance*: Availability of entities and facilities to strike work-life balance; health and fitness programs; stress reduction program; availability or personal help and counselling

Critique on Hergberg

- Theory is simple and has many good features, but it falls short of pointing a clear set of directions for utilizing these motivators and demotivators to enhance motivation.
- Some of the ideas are outdated and are not directly applicable to workforce culture of today.
- Applicability to retention management is minimal.

A NEW PARADIGM OF GOAL-HIERARCHY

Goal satisfaction is the primary pre-requisite to worker happiness. And happiness induces motivation. A happy, motivated, and satisfied individual would, in all probability, be dedicated, faithful, and committed to the organization's cause.

Goal-fulfilment → Happiness → Motivation → Commitment → Retention

To understand these chains of events leading to job-permanency, it is, therefore, imperative to first clearly identify the goals and aspiration of today's workforce, and then try to develop a suitable framework for fulfilling those goals.

Developing such a need-hierarchy profile for today's individual is, indeed, by no means an easy task - we have to take into consideration many divergent sets of constraints. Consider the following difficulties:

- ▸ The goals of the individual are fluid in nature - they keep changing with: (i) changes in the socio-economic framework of society, (ii) the individual's personal situation and personal priorities.
- ▸ Changes in the business environment also keep occurring continuously. This makes it difficult to achieve a one-to-one matching between entities that are moving together, but at different speeds.
- ▸ Changes to business pressures and priorities and changing personal priorities make the task of need-hierarchy development quite difficult.
- ▸ Finally, we have the predicament of matching moving personal goals with fixed organizational goals of profitability and continued growth.

With this as the basis of our understanding, we are proposing a fresh new model of goal/need hierarchy of an individual reflecting today's business environment and its operating conditions. Based solely on experiential opulence, the subject matter has been developed from years of experience of having interacted and worked with people in a wide variety of situations, both in the public and private sectors.

A hierarchical progression of goals and expectations of today's individual follow, more or less, the following sequence:

1. Money
2. Work Environment
3. Work Itself
4. Self-Esteem
5. Security
6. Work-Life Balance
7. Advancement
8. Fulfilment

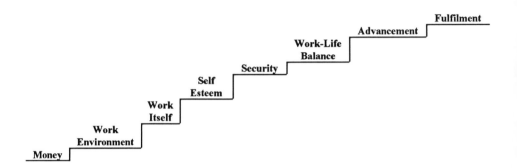

We shall now examine each goal in greater details, so that we can clearly understand what makes today's worker tic. How does the worker get motivated? What are the fundamental desires, that must be fulfilled before he/she would provide dedication and loyalty to the organization? The following discussion should provide us with sufficient ammunition to fuel the sense of motivation and self-discipline in the workforce.

1. Money

Although in today's affluent environment, money is not as important as it used to be a few decades ago, we would still like to put it as the first priority. Because it still remains a fact that a person's first aim in looking for a job is to provide sustenance - food on the table and a roof over his head. There is no person that we know of who is looking for a job that pays no money. Indeed, there are situations in which money may not be the primary factor, as for example:

- ▸ A person working as a social worker for community services.
- ▸ A person who has worked for many years and has enough money, but wants to keep himself busy doing something, and, therefore, working for a non-profit organization.

Since in this book we are not considering such situations, we would, therefore, wish to keep money requirements as part of the overall scenario.

We must make it clear that "money" is not an eternal goal - it is identified here only as a necessary entry-point requirement. Once this requirement is amicably and mutually agreed upon, it ceases to be a need - until of course, when this need reappears later in time in the form of the need for "advancement".

2. Work Environment

The next step starts from the context of the person being actually on the job. His first concern is about the work environment in which he has to work. This factor includes many aspects, such as:

- Relationship with peers and superiors
- Acceptance by the colleagues
- Interpersonal relations
- Company's attitude towards him

This is typically the first step of the need-hierarchy, after the pay has been settled and the job has been accepted. At this stage, the worker is looking for a pleasant and harmonious work environment, in which he feels comfortable, happy, and being gracefully accepted and wanted.

3. Work Itself

As soon as the worker finds the work environment amicable and conducive to his expectations, his next focus of attention is the nature of work itself. Following is a list of general attributes that an individual looks for:

- Is the work challenging?
- Does he have adequate tools, technology, resources and training to do his job?
- Are the processes and procedures adequate and helpful?
- Does he have sufficient control and ownership over his processes?
- Does he have appropriate responsibility and decision-making authority over the processes that are under his control?
- Does he have sufficient management support?
- Are the cross-functional support systems adequate?

4. Self Esteem

Once the worker finds both - the work environment as well as the work itself - satisfying, the next item on his wish list is self-esteem. Some of the entities on this list includes:

- Management support
- Recognition
- Praise
- Respect
- Credibility
- Peer support and recognition

5. Security

Having achieved the basic needs, the worker now likes to feel secure and wanted at the workplace. Job security helps to dissipate fear, enhances confidence, elevates sense of belonging, and improves worker's loyalty and empathy for the organization.

6. Work-Life Balance

By this time, the worker feels very satisfied and secure with his job, and he has achieved a higher level of maturity and consciousness. His appreciation of life and living reaches such a level that he begins to contemplate on life in the context of wholeness - of total life balance - of balancing personal and occupational life. He comes to a realization that work is not the end-all of life. Consequently, the worker begins to contemplate on the following:

- Am I utilizing my time proportionally and adequately to my on-work and off-work activities?
- How fulfilling is my personal and social life?
- Is the management sympathetic and helpful in my endeavours for work-life balance?
- What kind of facilities and infrastructure is available to me for work-life-health balance?

7. Advancement

This aspect of the worker's need hierarchy includes such entities as:

- Further training and development
- Opportunities for growth and advancement
- Greater responsibility
- Promotion to higher levels
- Pay increase

In terms of fulfilment of tangible needs, this is the last wish for the worker. At this stage, the worker is raising the question: "If I am capable, I am recognized , if I have been given added responsibility, my job performance is satisfactory - then why should I not be rewarded for that?". The original money-wish comes back again, this time eulogized with many other considerations - pay increase, promotion, greater responsibility, shares in the company' s profits, etc.

8. Fulfilment

This wish is much like the euphoric meditative state - a state of higher consciousness. After the individual has all that he could ask for, he is still looking for the most important entity - fulfilment and total satisfaction. In fact, this state is so important that it can be the first and primary need and aspiration of some individuals, especially in today's affluent and highly conscious socio-economic environment. Everything that an individual has can become meaningless if he doesn't have job satisfaction and work-life fulfilment.

Finally, before we close this discussion of need-hierarchy, we would like to reassert as we did earlier, that this is one possible scenario of the sequence of goal-hierarchy for the individual. It is by no means the only one. Each person is motivated by different entities depending on his personal situation and personality characteristics. For example, some individuals may value self-esteem more than anything else, while others may look for pay increase and advancement as the primary objective. We have developed this sequence of goal-hierarchy from our personal experience and have noted that this overall framework fits a large proportion of the working population.

6

ANATOMY OF MOTIVATION

MOTIVATION: A WAKE-UP CALL

Now we come to the most important aspect of human business management - human motivation. Motivation is, undeniably, the single most essential entity required to achieve success, both at the occupational as well as personal levels. At the heart of every business activity, there is an intrinsic force and energy that drives the activity towards success and excellence - that intrinsic force is human motivation and endeavour. Virtually nothing can be conceived or realized without motivated human potential. Progress, prosperity, personal fulfilment - in fact, every aspect of our materialistic life owes its origins and advancement to human endeavour, ingenuity, and dedication - elements that are fuelled by human motivation. It is, therefore, no wonder that there is hardly any subject that commands so much unremitting attention as human motivation.

So far so good - we all understand how important motivation is for improving productivity or for retention management. What is puzzling is that how come, despite our best efforts and intentions, our motivation programs fail to achieve sustainable success?

In this chapter, we are taking a direct aim at this enquiry, and outlining some simple, but candid, explanation for this paradox. At the same time, a totally fresh look at this old issue is propounded, with some new paradigms that may help to achieve lasting results.

At each stage, we can look back and remember things we did or did not do, and wish we had "known then what we know now". This routine process is a normal part of business life. Unfortunately, most organizations tend to learn from the past, by which time they have already suffered a great many bumps and bruises. Wouldn't it be nice to know the pitfalls early enough so as to avoid system failures in the first place. Being cognizant of why systems fail can often provide the most conducive and powerful strategic framework for implementing a fail-proof system in the first place. From a personal experiential perspective of having dealt with many systems in various companies and organizations around the world, both in the private and public sectors, I have come to realize that the most predominant reasons for the failure of many motivational enhancement efforts relate to the following:

- A general lack of understanding what motivation really means, its nature and characteristics
- Our general system management deficiencies and idiosyncrasies
- Management's faulty perceptions and erroneous approaches to motivation enhancement
- A lack of self-directed impetus among workers for motivating themselves

We shall expound at length on these aspects in this and the proceeding chapters. My purpose is simply to provide a wake-up call - this one being on our own idiosyncrasies that ultimately plague the system. We are hoping that this information about the mishandling of our motivational efforts, however unintentional, would provide a positive feedback for building a more effective motivation program. The narrative is simply meant to provide food for thought - to look back and self-assess the strengths and weaknesses of our past actions - to gainfully utilize our experiential wisdom to create better systems.

TOWARDS A DEFINITION OF MOTIVATION

Since a large majority of the time, motivational efforts fail to produce tangible results because of a general lack of understanding what motivation really means, let me first outline some of the commonly used definitions and connotations surrounding motivation. The word motivation is much like the word "stress" - a profoundly fashionable term that has become an integral part of the popular lexicon. Yet, it has as many meanings and interpretations as there are people who experience it. A good starting point in understanding motivation may be to look up its dictionary meaning. There are four associated words that we should consider here: **Motive, Motivate, Motivator, and Motivation.**

- Motive is the root word for motivation - it implies a need for desire that causes a person to act to fulfill the need.
- Motivate means to activate, arouse, cause, drive, impel, induce, inspire, move, prompt, provoke, stimulate.
- Motivator is one who induces motivation. A motivator can be a person or an entity. As a person, the motivator can be either a manager motivating the

worker or a worker motivating himself/herself. As an entity, a motivator can be any reason, need, desire, or motive.

▸ Motivation is a condition of being motivated. It also implies ambition, desire, drive, inspiration, interest, wish, impulse, incentive, inducement.

Thus, a motive, acting as a motivator, motivates a person to achieve motivation.

Motivation = Motive + Motivator

Clearly, therefore, we can see that the most important entity in the process of motivation is the "motivator". This emphasizes the fact that in any motivation program, the following three factors play a crucial role in enhancing motivation:

▸ Management's efforts and abilities to generate worker motivation
▸ Individual's personal drive for self-motivation
▸ A viable motive or reason for the workforce to get motivated

These three aspects would become the focus of our discussion in the remainder of the book. But before we begin our anatomical autopsy of the subject, there is just one more task at hand - to establish the right perspective for the subject.

Motivation is something to do with the drive within an individual. When the drive is awakened and the person is motivated, it means he is ready and willing to utilize his capabilities to achieve optimum levels of performance. This indicates that motivation, by itself, is a meaningless and inert entity - that is to say, it is not the motivation itself that does anything - it is that we wish to be motivated so that we can do something else better - the important entity still remains there - "us" - we are important - we are the centre piece. Our efforts must, therefore, be focused on us - on how we perceive things and how situations are presented to us - how to create a harmony between our perceptions and reality - how to convince and awaken our inner psyche - how to help us to become self-driven. This is something that we must clearly understand in order to comprehend the vast vagaries of motivation. It should be clearly understood that motivation is not an entity or product that we can tangibly see - in fact, it doesn't have its own identity - it is simply a drive inside us, generated by our feelings and attitude. So, our motivation programs are not meant to improve motivation per se - they are meant to improve our feelings, which would awaken that drive within us to be motivated.

Continuing with our definition of motivation, let us now look at some of the most commonly encountered interpretations that people attach to the word motivation. The following table presents a succinct summary of the various connotations around motivation.

MOTIVATION: DEFINITIONS
Motivation means that: ▸ Employees are highly productive. ▸ Employees are managing their time effectively. ▸ Employees are self-starters. ▸ Employees are self-disciplined. ▸ Employees are creative and innovative. ▸ Employees have a positive attitude. ▸ Employees are proactive. ▸ Employees are dedicated ▸ Employees are cooperative and supportive. ▸ Employees willingly participate in team efforts. ▸ Employees willingly accept responsibility. ▸ Employees are responsible and accountable. ▸ Employees share the organization's vision. ▸ Employees are proud of being part of the organization. ▸ Employees have a good rapport with management. ▸ Employees feel empathetic towards the welfare of the organization.
My definition of motivation: ▸ **Motivation is all of the above put together.**

What conclusion can we draw from so many diverse interpretations of motivation? One thing is indeed clear, that motivation does not only pertain to a single solitary characteristic, but it is a multi-faceted entity. That is to say, motivation is a collective whole comprising of many requisite attributes put together as one unit, such as : higher productivity, sense of responsibility and accountability, proactive attitude, creative-mindedness, self-discipline, etc.

A FRESH LOOK AT MOTIVATION

In line with the humanistic mindset and premise of our book, we would like to define motivation a little differently - in a more humanistic manner. *Motivation, to us, is some kind of inner feeling, energy, or driving force inside our guts, that propels us to do our virtual best to achieve excellence in whatever we do.* There are three important characteristics one must have to achieve motivation: Desire, Attitude, and Responsibility.

MOTIVATION = DESIRE + ATTITUDE + RESPONSIBILITY

- ▸ You must have the desire to be motivated.
- ▸ You must have the proper attitude towards motivation.
- ▸ You must accept responsibility for generating motivation.

Desire = Energy - Drive - Will - Determination - Enthusiasm - Happiness

Attitude = Mindset - Proactive Behaviour - Positivity - Staying Power - Passion - Courage

Responsibility = Self-Discipline - Commitment - Empathy - Accountability - Dedication

And most importantly, motivation is a joint venture - a shared responsibility for both parties - the management and the workers. It shall never happen without their collective commitment. A perfect analogy to this is the following old saying:

> **You can lead a horse to water, but you can't make him drink.**

Let us elucidate this fresh concept of motivation and of shared responsibility through the following two paradigms:

Paradigm #1: Role of the Individual: The Paradigm of "Personal TQM"

The worker must be a full participant to the whole exercise, for after all it is he/she we are trying to motivate. We are annotating it as the paradigm of "Personal TQM (Total Quality Management) - a paradigm for making the horse drink willingly - evoking a desire within the individual to self-generate motivational threshold - to strive for self-discipline and total self-management - to expand his horizon towards the pursuits of excellence and fulfilment.

The details of Personal TQM shall be elucidated in a later chapter. For the moment, we can succinctly say that:

- The worker must have the inner desire and willingness to be motivated - the horse must want to drink.
- The worker must be predisposed to being motivated.
- The worker must himself generate positive behaviour and attitude to inculcate motivation.
- The worker must accept appropriate responsibility for achieving the state of self-discipline and self-management.

Paradigm #2: Role of the Management: The Paradigm of "Management TQM"

Without the management's genuine input, the worker shall never achieve the fullness of a heightened state of motivation, irrespective of how self-driven he/she is. The management's help, support, and leadership is virtually indispensable. We are annotating this aspect as the paradigm of "Management TQM (Total Quality Management)" - and the subject is elucidated further in the next few chapters. Thus:

- The management must provide viable reason and purpose for motivation - the horse must have a reason to drink.
- The management must create suitable infrastructure and working milieu to augment and reinforce continual motivation.
- The management must bear the responsibility for providing effective leadership to induce motivation.

WHY DO SYSTEMS FAIL?

Let us now turn our attention to some of the key factors responsible for the failure of many systems. Having been personally involved and associated with many diverse systems and situations, specifically relating to quality/productivity, I have been able to collate a set of key factors that I have observed to be instrumental in the demise of many systems and programs, including motivational programs. An understanding of these factors should provide a clear picture of what pitfalls to avoid in developing and managing a viable system. Firstly, in this section, we shall outline some system management deficiencies in general, and then in the next section, we shall highlight some major shortcomings relating specifically to motivation programs.

What is a system? A system is simply a sum total of activities and processes. The success or failure of a system is dependent on a variety of diverse factors and circumstances. Normally, a system rarely fails because of a single factor or blunder - the failure is a consequence of a collective impact of many factors and mistakes - small and large.

A motivation program is normally a part of some larger system. When a virus attacks a system, its effect permeates onto every part of the system, including motivation. Therefore, the viability of motivational efforts should always be evaluated integratively within the confines of other larger systems. In the same token, a system rarely succeeds because of a single magical act - the success comes through the collective impact of many initiatives and efforts of varying scale and degree, engendered on a continuous basis. Now we shall make a summary presentation of our findings of some key factors that bear profound influence on the success and sustainability of a system. Once again, like before, I must warn my readers that I am going to be rather brutally candid in my presentations.

KEY FACTORS LINKED TO SYSTEM FAILURE

System selection

One of the main culprit in system failure relates to the way we develop or select our systems. There are two ways a system can be developed: bring in a ready-made system from external sources, or build an in-house customized system. Indeed, the later of two options is better - because, when people build their own system with their own customized knowledge and experience, the system has much greater chance of success and sustainability. However, unless such a system has full participation and support of everyone in the organization, and unless the system is effectively monitored and controlled, it can easily fail.

More importantly however, it is the borrowed systems we want to warn about. Ready-made systems from external sources can be gainfully used as long as we use them intelligently. People within the organization who are to use these systems, must be given the authority and controls to customize the borrowed systems vis-a-vis their requirements. If you force yourself to operate and drag yourself within the confines of a system that is foreign to your operability framework and culture, system failure is bound to occur.

System Flexibility

The next problem is system flexibility - whether we build our own system or use a borrowed system. Our systems are generally too rigid, and overly structured - there is very little flexibility. Systems have to be flexible in two ways: flexibility to accommodate changes in the business environment, internal as well as external; and flexibility in terms of controls over the system - that is, people having control over the system operability - to be able to make any requisite adjustments or realignments to the system as the need dictates. We generally become slaves to the system - the system drives and dictates us - we end-up being pawns in a huge game of chess in which we were not invited to play. Let me give you a real-life example from my personal life. This is going back about 25 years - my organization had purchased the rights for the implementation of a system - there is no need for me to name the system - it was a good system, of course. Everyone in the organization, at least the key managers, were sent for a 3-day training to learn the system. When we came back, we were all supposed to rigidly follow the system, its principles, procedures and even the forms and proformas. In many parts of the organization, it was not too difficult to follow the system rigidly. But, in some areas, due to the distinct nature of work, it was virtually impossible either to follow the system in its present format or to utilize the proformas and forms imposed upon by the system. Unfortunately, my shop was one of those. And behold, I was not allowed to alter or change the forms, much less the system, to be able to apply the system to my needs. As a junior manager who did not want to lose his job, I struggled with the system in its rigid format for a few years until God heard my prayers, and the whole system died its natural death. I am using the word natural, because most systems like this either have a limited shelf-life or you virtually cannot carry on a big undesirable load on your shoulders for a long time - you are bound to drop it. Long life and good health is only possible when systems are people-developed, people-driven, and people-managed.

System Simplicity

Simplicity is the key to success. But, unfortunately we get a kick in establishing extravagant systems with lots of fanfare. Perhaps, systems with big, showy framework looks more elite and respectful. But, extravagance costs money and time - and how far can you go by expending resources unchecked. Under the veil of systems like this, people get engrossed in things like: buying new computers; printing gaudy looking forms and file folders; sticking to a schedule of meetings even when there is nothing to discuss; spending money on travels; spending money on off-campus meetings; ensuring that there are a lot of pizza parties or barbecue get-togethers; spending money on flyers and displays; and on and on - the business is centred around the logistics rather than around the purpose for which the system was established in the first place. People get busy in administering the system rather than worrying about the purpose of the system. And when the money runs short, which, of course, was bound to happen sooner than later, the bubble bursts and the program is abandoned due to lack of funds.

System Commitment

Another idiosyncrasy relates to our short-term commitment span to the system. You will laugh when I tell you this real-life happening - in one organization, I asked a person if they had a good TQM (Total Quality Management) system in place - the answer was: oh! TQM - yes - we used to have it - it started in 1996 and finished in 1998. Somehow, we uphold that uncanny assumption that systems and programs have a limited shelf-life - they must begin and end at a pre-stipulated date. We eulogize our programs and systems as time-bound projects and allot a fixed set of resources for the project. And naturally, we expect the project to end at some point in time, or earlier if the resources get exhausted. In some special cases, we may extend and allocate more resources, but, once again, with a firm conviction that the program has to end one day. And the funniest part is, that we do it for all systems, including the motivation or quality system, even when we know that a motivation enhancement or a quality system must operate on a continuum - without the finish line.

System Expectations

We want results overnight - we have no time and patience to wait. Let's look at quality systems - we pretty well know that quality is a long-term perspective - it takes time to build quality in - that, quality is not an entity that you can buy and bring it in to implement - that, neither Rome was built in a day nor Japanese quality superiority sprung-up overnight. Yet, we rush into implementing quick-fix programs and start expecting profound improvements overnight. Instead, we encounter profound failure and frustrations overnight. When the results do not meet our expectations, we abandon the program and begin our search for another program that could produce instant miracles. Like this, we run from program to program, looking for a miracle that doesn't exist. I am going to recite another real-life story. I was supposed to give a seminar on TQM and ISO 9000 certification in an organization. The coordinator warned me that I should not use the buzzword "TQM" - because, he said, we have abandoned the TQM exercise, and we are now into implementing "re-engineering". During my seminar, I asked the participants if they could tell me the difference between TQM and re-engineering - and not surprisingly of course, the answer was - none whatsoever - both system are meant to improve quality. Then, how does it matter, I said, whatever name or connotation we use for quality improvement. But, unfortunately, that's not the case, especially in North America - where we have an obsession to change the buzzword every five years or so - we cannot live with one buzzword for long. So much so, that in many government departments, there is continuous obsession to change even the names of sections and divisions or programs - as if, the change in name is going to change the focus or outcome - that never happens. What happens, of course, is that we instead end-up inducing an element of instability into the whole process.

System Empowerment

In this narrative, I am going to speak a bit against my own self - I am going to critique on the role of a consultant. When developing a system, the first thing we must do is to assess our internal resource capability to determine how far the system can be developed by our own people and how much outside help may be needed. If we need an outside consultant's help, we must make sure that our own people are fully committed and would provide full participation and input into the process from the beginning to the end - that is to say, the ownership of processes must remain in the hands of our people. The consultant should only act as a catalyst - a helper - to start the process, to provide knowledge-based experiential guidance and directions, and to carve-up a clear road map. But unfortunately, that doesn't happen - we empower the consultant more than our own people - we tend to leave everything in the hands of the consultant. People become uninterested and non-participatory - now that the consultant is here, he would do everything - we don't have to do anything - people exonerate themselves of all the responsibility. Except for a handful of people who are directly involved with the consultant, people at large become immune to the system. The system ends-up being the consultant's system.

The failure rate of systems with a scenario like this is generally very high - because, the builder (consultant) leaves and no one knows how the structure was built and what had to be done to maintain the structure. Surprisingly though, even when the workers were not properly empowered, when the system fails, the workers are held responsible and accountable for its failure. I have nothing against consultants - the point I am making is that the consultant should also vehemently emphasize to the management on the necessity of full worker participation, as well as the management should appropriately empower people and make sure that the workers at all levels of the organization are actively involved in the implementation process. There is no denying the fact that a consultant plays a very significant role - consultants generally have a very high level of focussed knowledge and ability to accomplish things quickly and efficiently - a good consultant can save you a lot of aggravation and wasted time and resources. However, the consultant should not take over everything in his own hands - he is only a temporary visitor there - he is going to leave one of these days anyway - he should build not only the system, but also the strength of the people to handle and carry on the system successfully. He should only act as a catalyst.

WHY DO MOTIVATION PROGRAMS FAIL?

The reasons responsible for system failure in general, as outlined in the preceding section, are also equally applicable to motivational programs. However, in this section, we shall now identify some motivation-specific aspects that exert enormous influence on the success of our motivation efforts. The following key factors responsible for system failure shall be considered in this section:

- Lack of understanding of what "motivation' really means
- Fallacy surrounding what "motivation" is expected to produce
- Lack of effective management input
- Lack of individual's inner desire, willingness, and efforts to become motivated
- Lack of collective interplay of efforts between the management and the workers
- Lack of viable reason for motivation
- Lack of constancy of purpose

LACK OF UNDERSTANDING OF WHAT "MOTIVATION" REALLY MEANS

One of the major impediment in the way of implementing and maintaining a successful motivation program is the lack of clear understanding of what motivation means and what to expect from a motivated person. Most organizations operate in a shrouded mystery of generalizations about motivation. No clear set of specifications are explicitly stated and no one knows with any certainty: what to expect from a motivated person; how would the impact of motivational efforts be tangibly measured; and what aspects or characteristics of a person would or should be augmented through motivational efforts.

The impact and contribution of a motivation program can only be viably assessed in relation to the past performance of the individual. For instance, to say that a person is highly motivated, we should be able to clearly decipher exactly what the person has done or achieved to give us the impression that he/she is motivated. To meaningfully evaluate the degree and extent of motivation, it is, therefore, important to know:

- What is the person's current level of productivity and how can we tangibly measure it?
- What was the person's productivity level prior to implementing the motivation program?
- What is the person's capacity and capability?
- What is the person's optimum achievement level?
- What is the person's level of training, knowledge, and experience and what impact it has on his productivity level?
- What impact does the current operating conditions have on the person's motivation?
- And finally, how can we tangibly measure the motivational improvements made, because of the program implementation?

This is just a sample of questions which must be probed in order to get a meaningful assessment of the impact of any motivation program. Although, many of these questions are subjective in nature and are difficult to quantify, yet we must attempt to focus our evaluative efforts around these types of queries so as to be able to formulate a tangibly concise strategy.

A second problem relating to motivation emanates from the fact that a large majority of managers associate motivation to higher production level. They envisage a person to be highly motivated if he/she starts producing twenty widgets per hour as against six that he/she was producing before. This sort of assessment has two serious drawbacks:

- Motivation, in this sense, only represents a single attribute - higher production. A single attribute, ie., production level, does not constitute the overall framework of motivation. Motivation is a sum total of many attributes and not just one. Also, higher production cannot be necessarily equated to higher productivity.
- Turning to the example of widgets, even in this limited sense of motivation, the differential between six and twenty widgets has to be meaningfully evaluated vis-a-vis the following:
  - What is the person's true optimum operability level? When producing six widgets, was the person operating below his capacity? If so, was it due

to lack of motivation, inadequate training, or unavailability of proper tools or technology? How do we now know that twenty widgets is his/her optimum level?

- Are twenty widgets produced with poor quality better than six widgets with superior quality? Is quantity more important than quality?
- Do we wish to enhance motivation for just one characteristic, viz, higher productivity? Or, do we wish to induce motivation for the improvement of a whole spectrum of attributes of work life.

The point we are making here is that organizations must formulate a clear picture of the totality of aspects associated with motivation before embarking on a motivation program. Motivation is a subject of profound difficulty by its own right, and if we do not clearly understand what exactly do we want in terms of motivation, the chances of achieving sustainable levels of success would be almost negligible. The items that deserve considerable thought while developing a motivational framework include, as a minimum, the following:

- ▸ What does motivation mean to us?
- ▸ What do we expect to accomplish by enhancing motivation?
- ▸ How could we tangibly measure the impact of motivation?
- ▸ How would we assess the extent of improvements made?

FALLACY SURROUNDING WHAT "MOTIVATION" IS EXPECTED TO PRODUCE

Another issue that jeopardizes our motivational efforts relates to our unrealistic expectations about motivation. Normally, when implementing the program, most organizations make an uncanny assumption about the current level of motivation to be minimal (close to 0%), and then immediately after the onset of the program, they begin to expect miracles (around 100% motivation). The basic assumption seems to be that the need for implementing the program has arisen because of the fact that the current motivational level was very low. And the expectation is that the program is going to turn ordinary workers into super-humans overnight.

In the end, unfortunately, miracles do not happen, because they were not meant to happen overnight anyway. The result is that the organization gets disgusted and the management starts blaming either people or the system. The program is abandoned and the search begins for another better model. In this manner, organizations jump from one model to another in search of an unrealistic miracle.

What lessons can we learn form these idiosyncrasies?

- ▸ In any organization, the current levels of motivation are never as low as some manager may envisage; if they were, you could not have been running your business until now.

▸ It is virtually an impossible task to quantify, with any degree of accuracy, the magnitude of the current levels of motivation.

▸ Motivation programs need time and patience to realize any meaningful levels of success. No program can produce results overnight.

▸ Motivation is not a phenomenon that starts from zero and shoots up to a hundred - if you can realize anywhere between 10 to 30% improvement, you should consider yourself to be lucky.

▸ Programs do not produce results - people do. Don't let programs drive people, let people drive the program. The ownership of processes must be in the hands of people. Focus on the people.

▸ Blaming people or program is no remedy to solve a problem nor is it an excuse to abandon the program.

▸ Jumping from one program to another in search of a miracle would not rectify the problem. There are no miracles out there. A system is what you make of it. By itself, a system is only an inert entity.

▸ Motivation is a people-dependent phenomenon - it need continuous reinforcement and dedication to motivate people.

LACK OF EFFECTIVE MANAGEMENT INPUT

A major shortcoming in our present day motivational efforts relates to insufficient management participation in the program. Most managers indeed do participate actively in the development and implementation of the program, but once the program is implemented, they inadvertently, and perhaps unintentionally, withdraw their active support and participation. With nobody to lead and induce enthusiasm on a continuous basis, the program comes to a grinding halt. Continuous management involvement in the motivation program is paramount to the success and sustainability of the program.

Since this particular aspect is very important in our discussion on motivation, the subject shall be expounded at length in the chapter on "Management TQM".

LACK OF INDIVIDUAL'S INNER DESIRE AND WILLINGNESS TO BE MOTIVATED

We have repeatedly emphasized throughout our discussion that the nucleus of all activities pertaining to motivation is the individual person - and that no motivational effort can succeed unless the individual is willingly desirous and predisposed to being motivated. It is possible that over the short-term period, an individual may be coerced, manoeuvred, or convinced to be motivated, however, for sustainable levels of motivation, the individual's own inner dedication and commitment is vitally important to the overall process.

This aspect of motivation, which we are annotating as "Personal TQM" shall be expounded at length in another chapter.

LACK OF COLLECTIVE INTERPLAY OF EFFORTS BETWEEN THE MANAGEMENT AND THE WORKERS

Many motivation programs suffer due to lack of collective cooperative effort between the management and the workers. Managers expect workers to motivate themselves, with little or no input from management. Workers, on the other hand, expect management to initiate and induce motivation. Each party puts the onus and responsibility for motivation onto the other.

Motivation is like a clap - it needs two hands to do it - management as well as workers. Each party has a unique role to play and has a distinct set of responsibilities towards the process. No motivation program can survive without the collective interplay of efforts of both parties.

After all, what is an organization - it is simply a sum total of individuals? A portion of this flock is known as management, while the other part as workers. However, this differentiation is merely a resultant of the difference in nature and extent of responsibilities. For the overall success of the organization, however, every person in the organization, irrespective of its hierarchial level, is indeed equally responsible, individually as well as collectively, for working towards the common mission of success. The same holds true for a motivation program.

LACK OF A VIABLE REASON FOR MOTIVATION

Everything we do revolves around a purpose, whatever the purpose may be. A purposeless life is totally demeaning and dehumanizing. No system can survive without a purpose. The same holds true for motivation.

Employees at every level of the organization require a valid purpose for their work. It is virtually unthinkable to expect workers to get motivated without a reason. The reason can, indeed, be anything, such as:

- Good working conditions
- Opportunities for growth and development
- Opportunities for decision-making
- Good management support
- Suitable incentives and rewards

Workers always need to establish and maintain a continuous cognitive association between the purpose and action in order to remain viably motivated. Managers at all levels must, therefore, endeavour to generate a suitable framework of reasonable and achievable goals for workers.

LACK OF CONSTANCY OF PURPOSE

Last but not the least, many programs fail because of insufficient long-term focus and constancy of purpose. Most organizations establish motivation programs as a special separate entity with minimal integration with the mainframe strategic business plan. Programs are envisaged to have a limited shelf-life, and, consequently, interest and activity surrounding the program also becomes short-lived. The program dies its natural death after a while. Then, after a long period of hibernation and inactivity, interest suddenly awakes again and management starts the process of developing and establishing another motivation program all over again. With intent remaining the same, and management still lacking in constancy of purpose, this intermittent interplay of efforts does nothing more than jeopardizing the integrity and seriousness of the program.

Motivation efforts cannot be encapsulated within the time limitations of a program - it is something to be operated on a continuum. You cannot, for example, expect to jog only for one day and expect its effect to last for two weeks. Motivation exercise and message must be continuously repeated, because the message has the tendency to fade away quickly.

In fact, this lack of constancy of purpose plagues many other facets of business operability. The one worth mentioning, as a parallel example, relates to the exercise of "restructuring" that most companies undergo. Most companies continue to spend resources unchecked for years and years. Suddenly, when things start going seriously wrong, they wake up to the fact that they need to assess the company's total operability framework, including such entities as: the nature and extent of direct and indirect costs and expenditures; effectiveness of resources - human, physical, and financial; state of worker motivation; competitive marketability; profitability, etc. At this point in time, they start undertaking profound restructuring. This generally involves taking drastic actions to realign the business activity. Unfortunately, the whole exercise creates serious morale problems, causes disruptions in the smooth and natural flow of business, and costs the company heavy losses in terms of productivity as well as market credibility. The whole exercise, perhaps sometimes, does more harm than good. A further irony is that after the exercise is over, the company once again quickly reverts back to its older routine of unchecked spending spree and continues this modus operandi until its next craze for restructuring.

The solution to this and all other similar problems is not so difficult - I annotate it by "concurrent re-engineering". It is a process for challenging and appraising your operability on a continuous basis. By doing so, the company can avoid the once-in-five-year exercise of drastic reorganization, restructuring, or downsizing, and also avoid the unwanted side-effects of these processes.

SYNOPSIS OF THE LESSONS LEARNED

We shall now summarize the main features of the foregoing discussion to highlight the important aspects that need careful consideration:

- Clearly define for yourself what motivation means to you.
- What would you like to see augmented in the employees - some special attribute or an overall enhancement of work life?
- What do you expect to achieve through the program?
- What is lacking in the workforce at the moment that is prompting you to establish the program?
- When the program is implemented and running, what indicators would give you the feeling that the program is achieving what it was supposed to achieve?
- How would you measure the effectiveness of the program?
- How would you know that an employee's motivational level has improved?
- Do you have a clear idea of the current level of motivation of employees?
- What aspects of work life would you like to see augmented through the motivational enhancement efforts?
- Do you have any idea about the optimum level of operability of workers?
- Do you have any idea about the optimum level of suitability of work for each employee?
- Do you know about the employee's level of capability and capacity to do the job?
- Do you know the level of training, education, and experience of your workers vis-a-vis the job they are doing?
- Have you given the employees the purpose for their work and for motivation?
- Motivation comes through an employee's inner dedication and commitment. What steps have you taken to awaken the psyche of the individual to inculcate the inner desire for motivation and self-discipline?
- Have you adequately prepared management to play an effective role in motivating the workforce?
- Is the organization and its management committed to the program?
- Is the program customized, user-friendly, and manageable?

▸ Does the program have adequate involvement of the workers, as well as the management?

This is just a sample of some of the important aspects that require careful consideration during the implementation and maintenance phases of the motivation program. The success of the program is totally dependent on the collective cooperative effort of the management and workers working towards a shared vision.

MOTIVATION AND COGNITION

We shall now touch upon a rather new subject area - " *the science of cognition*" - to study the process of attitude formation and its impact upon motivation. As asserted earlier, we know that a happy worker is a motivated worker. But happiness is a by-product of attitude. It is, therefore, apropos to find out how individuals formulate their attitudes, what factors impact attitude formation, and how can we exercise interventions and controls over work-life situations which influence an individual's thought processes.

To study this aspect, we shall study human behaviour from the cognition standpoint. Although the principles of cognition have had limited applications to date, the subject is, however, gaining good momentum and credibility for applications to many diverse fields of study. Because attitude formation is a resultant of cognitive processes, we are attempting to introduce this new application of cognitive principles to the study of motivation enhancement.

First, let us locate the place where cognitive processes occur. In our brains, there are two important areas: the cerebral cortex, or the neo-cortex, and the limbic region. Cognitive analysis operates in the neo-cortex, while the limbic system stores our feelings, emotions, and value system. However, there is a high degree of correlational inter-dependence between our cognition and the emotive reactions of the limbic system.

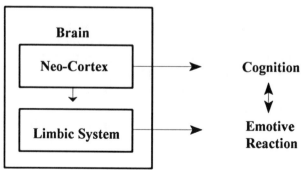

Let us examine how the two systems operate. **Cognition** pertains to awareness, judgement, and perception of reality without subjective bias. The process begins when we perceive a given situation and make a subjective evaluation of what it is and what it means in relation to our circumstances, beliefs, and values. If it is in conformity with our beliefs and expectations, we would be happy - have a positive attitude - and be more susceptible to motivation. If not, then we would exercise one of the three options: accept it as is; re-evaluate and make readjustments; or challenge it.

The limbic system, on the other hand, maintains our feelings, emotions, and value system. It's a storehouse that empties itself or fills itself continuously in accordance with our reactions to the day-to-day situations.

Both systems, however, exert influence on each other. Our cognitive evaluation, howsoever supposed to be unbiased, would be affected by the state of our limbic system. Our limbic system, which determines our behaviour pattern, is affected by what we see and hear. Note that since the cognitive processes operate on a continuum, our perceptual analysis is subject to continuous revision, and consequently, so is our emotive reactions.

Let us analyse the cognitive process further along with its relationship to the limbic system. Note the following observations:

▸ If we see and hear a wrong message, our cognition is bound to draw wrong conclusions - leading to formation of a negative attitude, resulting into motivation problems. So the first important lesson for the management is to convey the right information to the workers.

▸ However, even if the message is right, our cognition is still going to match the conclusions against our beliefs residing in the limbic system. If there is a high degree of concurrence between the two, we shall accept the perceptual analysis with a positive attitude, or else we will get into a state of internal conflict and dissatisfaction.

▸ If our limbic system, in itself, is preoccupied with some emotional state, as a result of prior thoughts or unrelated events, it would colour our perceptual analysis and we would tend to perceive the situation in a less realistic manner. How often, for example, we carry our anger and frustration from events that transpire at home, onto our working environment and indiscriminately show our anger on our colleagues for no obvious fault of theirs.

▸ Since the cognitive processes operate on a continuum, the conclusions we draw from our perceptual analysis can also undergo transformation. In the same token, the emotions, feelings, and beliefs in our limbic are also subject to re-adjustment with changing circumstances. To give you a real-life personal example, I remember, at one time, having a buffet lunch with some of my friends at a restaurant. I was thoroughly enjoying what I was eating. Suddenly, my friend Paul turned around and asked me if I knew what I was eating. Obviously, what I thought was chicken legs were in fact frog legs. Instantaneously, my feelings of enjoyment changed to disgust (I hate frog legs!). Thus, you can see that my cognitive appraisal of the situation (chicken legs) was positive and consequently, my emotive and behavioural reaction was in harmony with my value system. However, with additional factual information (frog legs), my revised cognitive judgement was unfavourable to my emotional feelings, and therefore, my behaviour was altered.

With this understanding of the cognitive processes, let us now establish an association between motivation and cognition. The way a worker perceives a situation, makes a mental picture and draws conclusions - determines how he is going to react to the situation and what attitudinal pattern he would formulate. The worker would evaluate the available information against his personal needs and expectations and would draw conclusions about the viability and suitability of the working environment. If there is a high degree of compatibility between his cognitive perception and personal beliefs, he will formulate a positive attitude and would be very receptive to motivation. On the other hand, if the available information is insufficient or unreliable, his cognition is bound to make faulty assumptions. Indeed, it is true that, many a times, our judgements are biased in favour of our own interests. It is human nature to filter the information, through selective perception, in a personal way and draw conclusions that reflect our own viewpoint. Unfortunately however, perception at time being stronger then reality, the wider the gap between the worker's perceptual judgement and the reality of the situation, the greater would be the impediment in the way of motivation enhancement. How would you notice these gaps? Very easily - these gaps translate themselves into the moans and groans, and the rumours and murmurs that you can hear among workers in the corridors. Let us consider a few typical ones:

- ▸ I don't know what's management up to.
- ▸ Nobody tells me anything.
- ▸ They keep everything secret and well guarded amongst the management group.
- ▸ They are not committed to the system.
- ▸ They won't give me proper resources to do my job.
- ▸ I have no idea what's involved in the quality system, and who is responsible for doing what.
- ▸ No training has been given to us on how to manage the quality system procedures and processes.

- They never ask for my opinion.
- They are afraid to empower us with the responsibility to manage our own processes.
- They don't trust us.
- Why should I work harder - they are not going to pay me extra?
- I just keep doing whatever I am told to do - I don't ask questions.
- As long as I am doing whatever I am told - I have done my job.
- They don't really care for us.
- What have they really done for me?

Can you imagine what kind of motivation can be expected from an environment in which such negative perceptions, real or imagined, run rampant among workers. Before we analyse this scenario any further, I would like to express my amusement about this intriguingly funny connotation around the word "they" - so inordinately, but commonly used in these corridor murmurs in almost every organization. I guess when workers refer to "they", they mean "the management". The incongruity about the whole matter is that I have even heard managers saying: "they don't tell us anything". The eccentricity goes even further - I have heard even some senior executives, especially in the public sector, make the same complaint, "they don't tell us everything". Naturally, one wonders, therefore, who the "they" really are. These phrases and connotations may sound funny - but they are really a true and candid manifestation of a reality that is out there. We can surely draw some serious conclusions from this obviously funny scenario - that the prevailing negativistic atmosphere of the workplace is a clear indication of the following:

- Lack of trust at every level
- Absence of shared vision
- Lack of effective communication and information flow
- Lack of operational transparency

From the above discussion we can conclude that, our emotive reactions and attitude that we formulate through our cognitive evaluation of the situation at hand, are really the determining factors in our drive for motivation. We can utilize this knowledge to improve our motivation efforts in the following manner:

- Managers should endeavour to provide a true and complete picture of the constraints and predicaments of the organization. This can be accomplished through personal contact, group meetings, or through a team infrastructure.
- Managers should be sensitive to the needs of the individuals and their complaints, even including the corridor moans and groans - which, by the way, should not be discarded as trivial and meaningless.

- Matters should be systematically and amicably settled through group discussions and active cross-functional interface.
- Managers and workers should closely collaborate with each other on a continuous basis, at a hands-on level, to ensure that a common understanding of the system requirements permeates at all levels of the organization.
- Workers also have a very important role and responsibility to undertake - to ensure that they make unbiased and judicious cognitive appraisal about the reality of the situation; and they do not let their emotional reactions and attitude, housed in the limbic system, that are unrelated to the work environment, interfere with the unbiased judgemental activity of the cognitive process. This needs a good deal of practice, regimentation, and self-discipline to accomplish this task.
- Workers should freely and frankly discuss their concerns with the management with an open mind and positive attitude, and resolve any outstanding issues in a fair and reasonable manner.

MOTIVATION AND RETENTION

Let us summarize our findings and reassert the importance of the motivation-retention connection.

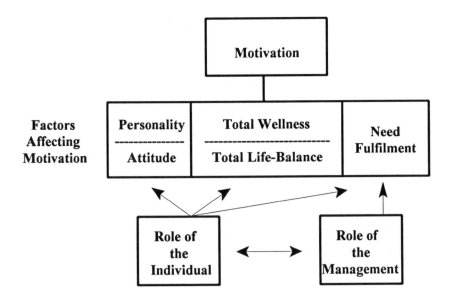

- ▸ Retention and long-term commitment comes through worker happiness and motivation.
- ▸ Motivation and fulfilment comes through the following:
  - Having a positive attitude
  - Achieving total wellness through total life-balance
  - Satisfaction of goals and expectations
- ▸ Management's role in motivation:
  - Understand the cognitive processes which affect attitude formation.
  - Provide accurate and timely information to the employees to induce unbiased cognitive appraisal leading to positive attitude.
  - Use various tangible and intangible means that lead to worker motivation.
  - Develop a goal compatibility between the worker's goals and the organization's goals.
  - Work towards worker's goal fulfilment to the extent possible within the framework of operational constraints.
  - Work towards the whole person wellness approach, rather than only the work aspects of a worker's life.
- ▸ Individual's role in motivation:
  - Inculcate a positive attitude by generating compatibility and harmony between your cognitive system and limbic system.
  - Accentuate self-management to achieve total life-balance.
  - Develop a goal compatibility between your goals and those of the organization.
  - Create a sense of responsibility and empathy for the organization.

PART 2

THE ACTION

7

GOAL COMPATIBILITY

INTRODUCTION

From the understanding phase, we now enter into the action phase. The preceding chapters were devoted to understanding the various facets of the HB management problem, and the associated entities that bear an impact on it, such as: the goals of the organization; need-hierarchy of the individual; the impact of changing business environment; and the role of human motivation in the equation of success. We came to the realization that when a worker feels unhappy, dissatisfied, and trapped in a situation, he becomes demotivated, resulting into loss of productivity - which, in turn, affects the organization's bottom line. And that, this dissatisfaction normally emanates from unfulfillment of the worker's goals and needs. Naturally therefore, our first obvious step should be to examine the goal hierarchy of the individual in greater detail, and identify the roles and responsibility of the management as well as the worker in their fulfilment. Indeed, while doing so, we also have to correlationally examine the goals of the organization to see what possible realignments can be made in the goals of both parties to minimize goal-divergency - so as to achieve goal compatibility. Accordingly, we shall undertake to do the following in this chapter:

- ► First, we shall study the origin of goal-incompatibility. For this, we shall go to the beginnings of the employment process.
- ► Then, we shall take the goals of both parties, one by one, and identify: the realities; the method of their fulfilment; and the roles and responsibilities of both, the management and the worker, towards their amelioration.

THE PROCESS OF EMPLOYMENT AND RETENTION

As briefly indicated earlier in the prologue, the process of employment begins with two parties, the employer and the individual to be employed, getting together to establish a working relationship. At this point in time, each party comes in with their own pre-established sets of goals and needs. Although, this is very normal of course, but the seeds of goal-divergency are sown right here. Let us examine the perspective of each party separately.

ORGANIZATION'S PERSPECTIVE

- The organizations is seeking for a person to fill a position for performing a designated set of tasks.
- The management has a set of specific goal and expectations for the individual, as well as they have their global mission of profitability and continued success. And they are expecting to find an individual who, while fulfilling the specific designated tasks, would ultimately be also responsible in achieving the organization's success mission.
- At this initial juncture of hiring, the organization has no concern or empathy for the individual's goals. No organization goes out to hire a person for the sake of satisfying the person's goals. Indeed, that may come in, if at all it does, at a later time in the relationship. At this point, however, the management has only their own self-centred goals in mind, and that is why they are bringing in the individual. It is not to say, of course, that they are not cognizant of the individual's goals. Surely they are. For, they want to lure a person to get the best available capability on board.

INDIVIDUAL'S PERSPECTIVE

- Likewise, the individual also has a set of goals and expectations with which he/she comes in while seeking the employment. The individual has many goals and needs in mind, but the main one at this juncture is to get the job, so that his basic physical and financial needs are fulfilled.
- Much like the organization, the individual also has no special empathy or feelings for the goals of the organization at this point in time. The individual is not coming in for a job interview with only the goal of the organization's welfare in mind - he/she is coming in for his/her own short-term needs and long-term goals.

So, as we can easily see from this brief characterization of the process of employment, the seeds of goal-divergency are embedded right at the beginnings of the process. Typically, this process is nothing more than a marriage of convenience between two parties, with each party entering into this matrimonial relationship with their own divergent set of self-centred goals. Obviously, therefore, both parties have to work hard to mellow this goal-divergency and incompatibility, for if left unchecked, it is bound to lead to the breakdown of the marriage of convenience, resulting into employee-employer divorce.

Both parties have equal responsibility in creating a goal harmony. If they fail to fulfil their obligation, it's a lose-lose situation for both. Although the organization faces a bigger loss, because they are left swirling around the process of hiring-retention-rehiring, which causes loss of productivity and unwanted expenditure of resources. But, the individual also feels the pinch of continued instability and unfulfillment. On the other end of the spectrum, however, if both parties make a genuine and concerted effort to be empathetic to each other's goals, then it is a win-win situation for both. The more an organization will look after the employee's happiness and satisfaction, the more the employee will provide his commitment, dedication, and loyalty to the organization's cause.

In light of this discussion, let us now examine the goals of the two parties collectively, and develop a goal compatibility framework. Recapitulating the goals identified in earlier chapters, appended below is a schematic of the goals of the organization and the need-hierarchy of the individual.

GOALS	
Organization	**Individual**
1. Productivity 2. Growth 3. Credibility 4. Profitability	1. Money 2. Work Environment 3. Work Itself 4. Self Esteem 5. Security 6. Work-life Balance 7. Advancement 8. Fulfilment

We shall now study these goals one by one and identify what roles both parties have to play to realize goal compatibility and fulfilment.

GOAL COMPATIBILITY ANALYSIS: ORGANIZATION

The first three goals of the organization - productivity, growth, and credibility - are accountable to and directed towards the fourth and primary goal of "profitability".

High Productivity → Continued Growth → Market Credibility → Profitability

GOAL #1: PRODUCTIVITY IMPROVEMENT

Productivity is the most essential element in the equation of success. Let us try to understand what productivity means, how to improve it, and what role management has to play.

In the simplest possible terms, productivity means: producing more with less. It doesn't, however, mean producing more of junk, at the cost of reduced workforce. It means, motivating the workforce so that they would produce more and better within the same or less timeframe and with less resources.

As a prerequisite to improvement, it is essential to gather a realization of the following entities:

- ► What exactly do we want to improve in a person?
- ► Do we know an individual's current level of productivity?
- ► Do we know an individual's capacity and capability levels?
- ► How much improvement do we expect to induce?
- ► Would we be able to quantify the improvement made?
- ► Is there a benchmark or global measure of improvement against which we can compare results?

Productivity is not a singular attribute - it is a resultant of the combined impact of many attributes - hardware, software, and humanware. To improve productivity, an organization needs to do the following, as a minimum:

- ► Enhance worker's motivation.
- ► Help the individual to develop self-confidence, and self-discipline.
- ► Provide proper tools and technology to improve production and productivity.
- ► Simplify processes and procedures to facilitate performance.
- ► Reduce bureaucratic barriers to effective decision-making.
- ► Provide the individual with better control of his processes.
- ► Provide challenge in the job.

- ▸ Help in the fulfilment of individual's goals and aspirations to the extent possible.
- ▸ Last, but most importantly, work towards improving the worker's performance mindset, to ensure that the worker:
  - • does not waste time consciously
  - • creates quality work
  - • accomplishes more and better consistently
  - • cooperates with others to create excellence
  - • is self-driven, self-motivated, dedicated, and loyal

GOAL #2: CONTINUED GROWTH

Continued growth is a by-product of several business initiatives and actions, as schematically elucidated through the following chain reaction:

Motivated Workforce → Higher Productivity → Better Quality → Competitive Pricing → Customer Satisfaction → Aggressive Marketing → Expanded Market Share → Continued Growth

The main ingredients for achieving continued growth are:

- ▸ Constancy of purpose
- ▸ Highly skilled, motivated workforce
- ▸ Quality excellence
- ▸ Continuous improvement

GOAL #3: MARKET CREDIBILITY

Continued growth through the maintenance of higher quality and better customer satisfaction automatically brings market credibility to the organization. Achievement of this level of success brings a total win-win situation for the organization: profitability for the company, happy stakeholders, and satisfied workers.

GOAL-COMPATIBILITY ANALYSIS: INDIVIDUAL

We shall now elucidate the need-hierarchy of the individual; establish its links with the goals of the organization; and highlight the roles and responsibilities of both parties towards the fulfilment of these goals.

GOAL #1: MONEY

As iterated earlier, this goal of the individual has two facets. It comes into play initially at the time of settling the employment agreement between the two parties. And once the agreement is accepted, this goals ends temporarily - until it reappears later in the shape of promotion or advancement. Here, we shall discuss the initial importance of this goal, because our handling of this goal even at this initial stage can have enormous repercussions on the ensuing working relationship and on retention management. Both parties have a role to play at this stage as follows:

Role of the organization

- To attract good people, the organization has to:
  - offer salaries compatible with the individual's education, experience, and skill level
  - offer competitive rates that other similar organizations may offer to the individual
- If the above option is not viable or feasible, then the organization must consider other additional perks or benefits to offset and compensate for the lower salary offering.
- In addition, the organization should try to identify and develop other means and avenues by which they can convince the individual that working for this organization is more worthwhile and beneficial than any other.
- It must be noted that if none of the above happens, and the individual accepts the job for any number of personal circumstances, such as financial desperation, change of scenery, etc., then there is possibility of apprehension that the relationship has started in bad faith. Such relationships whose beginnings are embedded in the feeling of coercion, desperation, and dissatisfaction, have a high probability of early breakdown. The individual in such a case would quit the job at the first possible opportunity he gets to land another better job somewhere else.

Role of the Individual

- It is also equally necessary for the individual to make sure that he doesn't begin his new relationship based on unreasonable expectations and demands. The individual must be sympathetic to the constraints and predicaments of the organization. For if that doesn't happen, the organization may be forced to hire the person due to desperation or operational urgency, but a relationship like this would have little chance of survival. For, as soon as the organization's immediate needs are fulfilled and urgency rectified, the organization would get rid of the individual, and find another suitable person with less or more reasonable demands.

GOAL #2: WORK ENVIRONMENT

Role of the Organization

- ▸ The organization have a high responsibility for creating a good working environment for the employees. A good working environment is such in which the workers feel: at ease, wanted, cared-for, happy, an integral part of the organization, at ease with management, and proud to be working for the organization.
- ▸ People want to do a good job, but they can only do so if they are provided with the right work environment.
- ▸ Good working environment can only be achieved by creating a proper organizational and operational infrastructure, such as:
  - process improvement teams
  - employee suggestion mechanisms
  - regular work meetings among the managers, supervisors, and workers, to discuss job-related and personal issues
  - regular meetings between senior managers and workers to resolve outstanding issues of both personal and occupational nature, and to listen to workers' concerns
  - motivation enhancement sessions

Role of the Individual

Just like the organization, the individual also has high responsibility towards making the work environment harmonious and gratifying. Some of the individual's efforts include such things as:

- ▸ keeping a pleasant and positive attitude
- ▸ participating in team efforts
- ▸ accepting challenge and responsibility
- ▸ be honest with people
- ▸ be pro-active in offering help and assistance
- ▸ be genuinely concerned and empathetic to the cause of the organization

GOAL #3: WORK ITSELF

Role of the Organization

The organization must endeavour to ensure that all work-oriented aspects are adequately provided to the employees so as to enable them to perform their duties with a high level of productivity and performance excellence. Examples include such entities as:

- adequate training
- proper machinery and tools
- element of challenge in the job
- room for innovation and improvement
- simplified procedures and processes
- effective support systems
- fast and unbureaucratic decision-making
- adequate and prompt availability of requisite resources
- control and responsibility within the hands of employees

Role of the Individual

The individual also has an important role to play, without which neither the work can be invigorating nor any of the management's actions can bring any viable results. The employee must:

- be self-driven
- be well-organized, self-disciplined
- be inquisitive and innovative
- be proactive and participatory
- continuously seek improvements in processes

Unless the individual exercises greater personal initiative, drive and commitment to make his work more invigorating, the work can quickly become a drag, leading to boredom, loss of interest, and lower productivity. And all of this can happen despite the management's best efforts to make work more interesting and challenging. The individual's own input is of paramount importance.

GOAL #4: SELF ESTEEM

This is the most important of the individual's goals in today's environment. Today's worker values "fulfilment" and "self-esteem" more than money on the job. Workers don't complain about salaries as much as they do about self-respect, involvement, openness, and treatment by the management. Today's workplaces are not really underpaid but dehumanized. Technology and computers have replaced the personal touch. While money is important, what motivates employees to achieve performance excellence is thoughtful personal kind of recognition that signifies true appreciation for a job well done. And as we have repeatedly said before, the extra effort by people is a function of how they are treated - and this softer side of management has the most potent power to induce motivation - and at the same time it is totally free.

This is where the management's input and capabilities play a significant role - in learning how to use the softer aspects of management - in caring for the individual - treating the worker like an internal customer - in making a subtle appeal to the worker's consciousness to improve productivity. And all of these efforts are, in a sense, for the benefit of the organization itself - because, a happy and satisfied worker is a productive and dedicated worker.

GOAL #5: SECURITY

Job security in an age of high mobility is not the main concern of an individual, yet most workers would like to be assured of a secured job in order to perform their duties peacefully and efficiently. A worker who lives under a constant fear of losing his/her job would never be able to achieve a performance mindset and empathy for the organization.

Normally, the job loss occurs as a result of the following situations:

- ▸ continued poor performance by the worker
- ▸ downsizing by the organization

In both of these situations, once again we can see that the management has to play an important role. To elucidate it further, let us consider each situation separately.

Poor Performance

Loss of job due to poor performance should never come to the individual as a surprise. It's an entity that should have been regularly discussed and clearly understood by both parties - the management and the worker. Poor performance can be due to several reasons, such as:

- ▸ person is not inherently capable for that kind of job
- ▸ person is not able to perform well because of poor training, lack of resources, poor technology, or inadequate procedures
- ▸ person is not motivated or self-disciplined

These and several other similar situations should be continuously evaluated by the management in consultation with the employee. Many of these deficiencies can be rectified, resulting into the employee performing better than expected.

Downsizing

Downsizing may at times be essential and the only option for the organization to survive and achieve financial stability, yet I personally believe that downsizing is a direct by-product of unplanned and unintelligent upsizing. Downsizing, in fact, does more harm than good - it creates dissention between management and workers - generates fear, insecurity, and instability - brings the morale down - lowers productivity in general.   Downsizing is not the answer for improving the organization's strategic health - "rightsizing" is.

GOAL #6: WORK-LIFE BALANCE

Work and life balance is an important concern for today's worker. Management has to accept this reality as the status quo and understand that personal life and occupational life are not competing but complementary. Today, when you hire an individual, you are not just hiring part of the individual - you are hiring the whole individual - you must not compartmentalize, but consider life-balance from the perspective of wholeness.

It needs collective concurrence of both parties to know what's expected, what's possible within the operational constraints, and what can be mutually accommodated. It requires creating a new partnership, in which goals of the individual as well as the organization are amicably met.

GOAL #7: ADVANCEMENT

Now we come back to the second half of goal #1 - the money goal. Though, at this stage the perspective is different - it relates to promotion, increase in salary, advancement, financial rewards, bonuses, etc.

This goal is very tricky, and for any hope of reconciliation between the management and the worker about this goal, each party has to clearly grasp the achievable and the non-achievable.

Management's Perspective

- ▸ Management's dilemma - they can neither afford to ignore the worker's aspirations, nor can they possibly fulfil all their demands and expectations.
- ▸ No organization can afford to continuously give pay increases and promotions to all employees at all times. Consider the following enigmas:
  - • if the organization keeps giving salary increases all the time, they would soon go bankrupt.
  - • it is not a good practice to associate productivity with higher pay - i.e. one happening only when the other happens.
  - • how can everyone be promoted to a higher level management position, when there is no room at the top - also, if everyone becomes a manager, there won't be any workers left.

> ► Management is doomed if they do, and they are doomed of they don't. Management must, therefore, devise some strategies to diffuse the situation. One way, as suggested earlier, is to attempt to transfer the individual's mental expectations of the tangible physical entities to the satisfaction of mental intangible expectations. That is to say, instead of concentrating on the satisfaction of physical demands like salary increase, promotion, etc., management should concentrate on satisfying the mental intangible needs such as: needs of self-esteem, work-life balance, recognition, praise, etc. Satisfaction of these intangible needs is as powerful as the satisfaction of tangibles. And most importantly, their satisfaction is totally cost-free and easily achievable.

GOAL #8: FULFILMENT

This goal is a sum total of all other goals. If the management has done their job well in satisfying the other goals of the individual, then worker happiness and fulfilment would come in by itself. If that happens, then we can at least say that management has played their role effectively. However, it should also be noted that, since satisfaction and happiness is a personal thing, the goal of fulfilment is equally dependent on a person's own outlook and attitude.

GOAL COMPATIBILITY SYPNOSIS

Following are some key points about goal compatibility that should be carefully noted:

> ► It is utterly imperative for everybody to realize, especially for the workers, that the organization's goals have the highest priority over everything else. Their fulfilment is virtually mandatory if the organization is to survive and succeed. The organization's goals of profitability are static and eternally unchanging. Because of their importance, there is really no need to make the organization's goals compatible with any other goals, including that of the individual, because they must be fulfilled.
> ► The organization is not mandated to fulfill all the goals of the individual in their entirety, though it is in the organization's own best interest to try to satisfy the individual's needs to the extent possible within the framework of their own goal fulfilment and operational constraints.
> ► Since the individual's goals are fluid in nature - i.e. they keep changing with time and from individual to individual - the organization must carefully attempt to understand them and align them with their own goals.

> It is the individual who has to understand that his/her goals must be made compatible with that of the organization, for they cannot uphold their own independent existence while being in opposition to the organization's goals. No organization would ever tolerate an individual whose goals are not compatible with those of the organization.

> Finally, however, we must emphasize that both parties must become equal partners in accepting responsibility for understanding each other's goals, being sensitive to each other's needs and to the passion for the satisfaction of their goals, and developing a sense of concern and empathy for each other.

Since the management holds all the trump cards of authority to do or not to do things, they have slightly bigger responsibility towards motivating the workforce. They must develop effective infrastructures of tangible and intangible means, efforts, and initiatives to fulfil the employee's needs. And doing this is, in fact, in their own best interest, because unless the individual is happy and satisfied, the organization's own goals cannot be fully realized. An unhappy worker would quit his job at the first possible opportunity he would get, and go to another organization who would be more sympathetic towards his needs.

In the unwanted situation of a breakdown of relationship between the two parties, both parties suffer - though, the organization's sufferings are a bit bigger. The individual suffers from instability and unfulfillment, but the organization suffers from loss of productivity, revenue, and the unwanted expenditure of resources resulting from the continuous headache of hiring-retention-firing-rehiring.

8

ON BECOMING A PERSON

A TRIBUTE TO HUMAN POTENTIAL

Systems, programs, and initiatives are an important and integral part of every business enterprise - there is no doubt to that, and we cannot do without them. However, when it comes to human motivation, we have to go a bit beyond the management of system logistics only - we have to concentrate our efforts also on the core competency of motivation - the human element. Instead of just creating and superimposing a well designed motivation program onto the individual to generate motivation, which of course will produce some temporary results, what we need to do is to develop the individual's strength and capability to achieve self-directed motivation that would be more permanent and lasting.

We have repeatedly asserted with unflinching personal experiential conviction and belief, that human potential is the ultimate force behind all of our achievements and success. History can provide us with ample testimony to that fact - we can look back into history, into any era, any culture, any society - and we would find that behind all success in any venture, it was the human person, the human potential, dedication, commitment, that was instrumental in achieving success. If that is too intricate to imagine, we can contemplate on the following rudimentary and simpler analogy:

- ▸ Machine produce quality, but who produces machines? People!
- ▸ Technology enhances our quality of life, but who develops technology? People!
- ▸ Money brings success to organizations, but who generates money? People!
- ▸ Excellence does not come by itself - who generates excellence? People!

So what we plan to do in this and the next few chapters, is to concentrate on the individual - the ultimate source of excellence. We would like to reach the psyche of the person - to undertake interventions to awaken that drive from within the person - to develop the person - to let the person himself create excellence. The next four chapters of the book are very unique - they are the theme chapters of the book, and they cover the following aspects:

- ▶ This chapter is devoted to personal growth and development. It outlines some golden rules to enhance oneself to become, what we call, a "person" - a good and efficient person - to achieve personal fulness and affability of life and living. The effort to achieve internal harmony is indeed totally the individual's own.
- ▶ In the next chapter, we wish to identify what this new and rejuvenated person have to do at the workplace to achieve success and fulfilment, both for himself/herself as well as for the organization. We are annotating it as the paradigm of "Personal TQM (Total Quality Management)". It is a call-to-arms to the psyche of every individual worker to rise above the ordinary - to set goals for themselves - and to give their personal best, individually and collectively, for the mutual welfare and success of both parties.
- ▶ Next, in chapter 10, we want to look at this "new person" in the context of a manager. We shall elucidate how to make this "person" a manager - and what are the attributes and qualities of a good manager.
- ▶ Finally, in chapter 11, we would identify the roles and responsibilities of this "new manager". We are annotating this as the paradigm of "Management TQM".

THE PERSON

A person is simply a sum total of three entities: body, mind, and consciousness. A large majority of our human business management programs and systems are directed to only one aspect - the body.

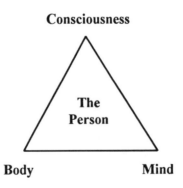

The tendency of these programs is to address the problem of human motivation through tangible initiatives only. That is why these programs become very expensive to operate and at the same time, they yield only temporary and lukewarm success. Throughout this book, we have recommended that management should also put their efforts in the intangible mental aspects of the issue, like: praise, recognition, respect, independence, etc. Such entities while being totally cost-free, make lasting impressions on a person's consciousness level, and are the most effective means of inducing motivation. But, we also asserted that no amount of organizational impetus can bring any lasting results without the individual's own willingness and determination to achieve higher realms of personhood. So, in this chapter, we wish to address this third aspect of the individual - the consciousness - the psyche. We shall present some simple ideas that a person can self-impose on himself to stimulate his inner self, in order to bring about a change or enhancement in his attitude and behaviour, and achieve self-confidence and self-discipline.

THE FULFILMENT

What is it that we want to achieve - a meaningful and fulfilling life? Without fulfilment, there is a feeling of emptiness in life - life is without meaning, dehumanizing - life is just a chore. We can go around in life, acting different roles, achieving temporary satisfaction and success - but, until and unless we are totally immersed in that euphoria of total consummation, there is no satisfaction.

Why do we need personal fulfilment? The answer is "why not" - it is everybody's birthright - we owe it to ourselves - and it is achievable. In fact, we need it for others also because our life is a continuous flow of interactions with others. If we are enriched and fulfilled, we will emit a positive aura and vibrations of happiness to whatever we interact with. And if we are unhappy inside, the negativity would not only affect us, but it would affect everyone else around us.

However, personal growth and enhancement is a very personal thing - it cannot come by itself - you have to have the desire and the will to bring it upon yourself. External forces can only provide a lending hand, but the main thrust has to come from within.

Total life fullness, affability, and fulfilment comes through total union with your existence, which involves the following:

- ▸ union with self
- ▸ union with your surroundings
- ▸ union with the laws of nature

Union with self is the starting point of "becoming a person". You need inwardly achievements in at least the following attributes (the 5 Cs):

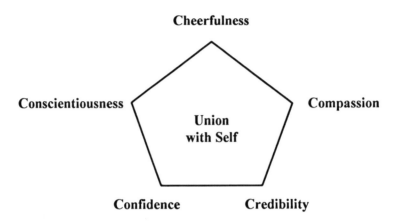

THE 5 CS OF BECOMING A PERSON

- ▸ Cheerfulness → happiness, contentment, fulfilment, enthusiasm
- ▸ Conscientiousness → honesty, dedication, diligence
- ▸ Compassion → empathy, kindness, respect
- ▸ Confidence → courage, self-reliance, trust
- ▸ Credibility → trustworthiness, integrity, dependability

Briefly speaking:

- ▸ You must be happy inside.
- ▸ You must be honest to yourself as well as to others.
- ▸ You must have compassion for yourself as well as for others.
- ▸ You must have confidence in yourself and in others, and others must have confidence in you.
- ▸ You must have personal integrity and others should be able to depend on you.

Union with the surrounding is the second step to achieving the so called "new personhood". Having achieved union with self, now you need to project that new self onto the environment around you to achieve a union with your occupational and social surroundings. The very basic characteristics required for this step are the following 5 Ps:

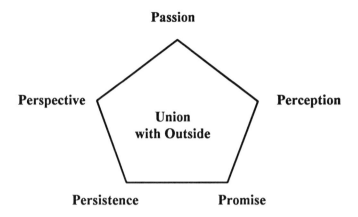

THE 5 PS OF PERSONAL PERFECTION

 ‣ Passion ➜ drive, desire, enthusiasm, assertiveness, strength
 ‣ Perspective ➜ attitude, outlook, thinking, behaviour, frame of mind, aptitude
 ‣ Perception ➜ awareness, consciousness, knowledge, capability, purpose, vision
 ‣ Persistence ➜ determination, discipline, forcefulness, tirelessness, constancy
 ‣ Promise ➜ commitment, dedication, responsibility, accountability

In summary:

 ‣ You must have passion in whatever you do.
 ‣ You need a positive attitude.
 ‣ You need knowledge to do things.
 ‣ You must have the determination to achieve the ultimate best.
 ‣ You must be self-disciplined and you must have the strength to take on responsibility.

KNOW YOURSELF

The process of union with the self starts with knowing yourself, you must completely and most honestly know the total you. For, if you don't know what you are, what you want, what you have, what you don't have - you cannot expect to make any meaningful personal realignments or mid-life course corrections? Also, if you don't know yourself, how can you expect others to know you and how can you expect to generate union either with self or with your surroundings?

The process of knowing the self begins with an introspective analysis of the self. It involves the identification of entities such as:

- ▸ your traits, physical and emotional
- ▸ your behaviour patterns
- ▸ your attitude
- ▸ the way you talk, smile, frown
- ▸ your gestures
- ▸ your strengths and weaknesses

AN EXERCISE IN SELF-ANALYSIS

We would like to present another naively simple exercise in self-analysis and self-improvement. The basis of the exercise is as follows: when you meet another person, you start analysing the person. You observe his movements; gestures; attitude; his behaviour patterns; the way he talks, smiles, listens, understands, and reacts. From all this observational data, you draw an overall picture of the person. Now, let us reverse the situation: when someone meets you, he is doing exactly the same to draw a picture about you - the way you behave, the type of person you are. So, the self-analysis exercise starts with finding what you are, and how people perceive you, or even how you perceive your own self.

THE EXERCISE

Everyday, spend a few minutes in your washroom, all alone, with doors locked. Look at yourself through the mirror, talk to yourself, and ask yourself the following questions:

- ▸ How do I look?
- ▸ Do I have a pleasant looking face, or do I look angry, unpleasant, or arrogant?
- ▸ Do I look honest, contented, confident, or do I look overly shrewd, dissatisfied, unsure, immature, or aggressive?
- ▸ Do I look happy or negativistic?
- ▸ Now smile - and see if your smile is pleasant and natural, or artificial and forcible.
- ▸ Now talk to yourself - and notice the tone of your speech and the gesture of your body movements. Is your tone aggressive, arrogant, or pleasant, mature, self-assured?
- ▸ Are your gestures comfortable or stressed?

- ► Ask yourself - how would people perceive me by looking at me and talking to me? What kind of impression would people form about me?
- ► How would I perceive myself, if I met myself on the street?
- ► What impressions do I have about myself?

These are some of the soul-searching questions that can provide excellent feedback. Make a checklist of the positives and negatives that you identify from this introspective analysis. Take each aspect identified in the checklist one by one and try to make improvements - for example - the way you smile and talk, your gestures, your facial outlook, etc. Continue the washroom visits, and keep working on those improvements bit by bit everyday. You will be amazed how much improvements you can make - even the way you look or present yourself. Remember, improvements won't come overnight - it takes time to correct the accumulated incorrectness of so many years. Once you achieve this improvement/transformation, you will be elated, and you will feel good about yourself - you will be simmering in that euphoric sense of internal happiness and contentment. You will attain the attainable - the total union with self.

PERSONAL IMPROVEMENT: THE GOLDEN RULES

In addition to the personal improvement attributes listed earlier, we shall now outline some golden rules for personal growth and enhancement, and describe how these entities can be activated to achieve fullness and enrichment of the self. Our explanation of each of the axioms appended below has been directed firstly inwardly to the individual, and then outwardly from the individual to his surroundings. We are intentionally presenting it like that, because we believe that first the individual has to bring about a transformation within his own self. And when he has achieved that inner state of higher consciousness, harmony, and life-balance - its effect will automatically flow over to the external environment with which he is routinely interacting.

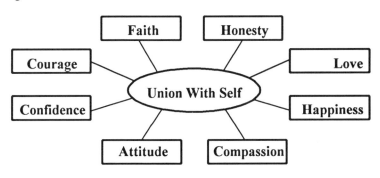

1. FAITH

- Faith is the most valuable commodity of the human species.
- The origin of faith is God. Our trust in God teaches us the meaning of the word faith.
- The first commandment, therefore, is: trust in God - even if it is not for religious connotations - which to me is also very important also. God provides us the steady foundation of our life - a meaning for our very existence. He is always there - always the same. Accept His grace. Communicate with him by prayer - prayer is the greatest miracle of the universe.
- Faith has two faces: faith in yourself, and faith in others.
- You must have faith in yourself, for if you don't have faith in your own self, how can anyone else have faith in you?
- Faith in yourself means: self-confidence; staying power; courage and conviction to accomplish things; courage to be different; courage to stand up and be counted; boldness; trust; self-reliance.
- You must generate faith in others too - for, if you don't trust others, you will be running amuck trying to do everything yourself.
- You must ensure that others can have faith in you also - which means they can trust you - they can depend on you.
- Faith provides stability and mental peace.

2. HONESTY

- Honesty is an important life attribute, both with yourself and with others.
- Honesty with others means that your relationship with them is one of: openness, decency, in good faith, straightforward, ethical, honourable, and equitable.
- Most importantly, you must be honest with yourself. For, if you are not honest with yourself, you can hardly be honest with anybody else. If you can cheat yourself, surely you would have no remorse in cheating others. Dishonesty with your own self would, in the long run, entail into a demeaning life.
- Consider a simple scenario of how an act of harmless dishonesty with yourself can rob you of your self-respect and trustworthiness. It's a work situation - you are doing some chores or sitting on your desk looking at some documents. Everyone gets the impression that you are very busy - you are working very hard. But really, you may simply be only gazing at the documents - you are physically there, but mentally you are somewhere else. You may be happy that you are wasting time. But, you don't realize that you are the one who is

being wasted - you are not wasting time, time is wasting you. Worse - you are not cheating anyone - you are cheating yourself - and the day you cheat yourself, that is the end of your meaningful life. For the sake of your own existence, you have to be accountable to yourself, if not to anybody else. Nobody else may be watching, but at least *you* are watching you. You have to be answerable to yourself. This is just one simple example of what honesty to yourself means. Honesty is the most important attribute for personal growth and enhancement.

3. LOVE

▸ Firstly, you must love yourself. For, if you don't love yourself, there is little chance that you will love others. Love life. Enjoy the beauty of life and living. It would infuse a sense of pleasure and happiness in you, and that would be immensely valuable for all other interactions of life.

▸ Love people around you - at home, at work, and outside. Love for others is essential for your own balanced life. The more you give of yourself, the more that will come flowing back to you. You will feel good about yourself.

4. HAPPINESS

▸ A happy worker is a dedicated, committed worker.

▸ Happiness is the ultimate passion of us all.

▸ But, happiness is merely a state of mind. Therefore, it is really up to us to inculcate that happy state of mind.

▸ If you are not happy, then the whole world will be doom and gloom for you. And certainly, you would not interact with others with a positive frame of mind and a pleasant and happy outlook.

▸ Contentment is the key to happiness. Contentment is also a pre-requisite for maturity.

▸ External events cause us anguish, discontentment, and stress. But, if we can learn to filter these through our internal screen of positive thinking, then nothing can bother us.

▸ Remember, we only get one trip through life. Grab hold of life, enjoy the trip, and leave some memorable footprints. Greet each day with a smile; the day will greet you back in the same manner. Love life. Be happy.

5. COMPASSION

▸ Try to be human - it doesn't need too much effort - because you are already human.

- Generate compassion and empathy for yourself and for others around you.
- Learn how to love and respect people and be sensitive to their feelings and emotion - just the same way as your own feelings and emotions.
- Learn how to forgive yourself, as well as others.
- Strengthen your relationship with others each day with love, care, support, and compassion.

6. ATTITUDE

- Attitude is a major contributing factor in human relations, especially in service-oriented organizations.
- Bad attitude affects motivational thresholds, job performance, relationship with colleagues, team participation - in fact, it affects every aspect of your home, work, and social life.
- But, attitude is a learned characteristic - it can be easily unlearned, relearned and corrected. It requires a complete harmony between your cognitive appraisals and feelings and emotions to improve attitude.
- With positive attitude, your work life, productivity, and general wellness can reach its optimum levels of excellence.

7. CONFIDENCE

- The first pre-requisite for growth and success is self-confidence.
- Think it this way: if you don't have confidence in yourself, how can others have confidence in you.
- When you lack confidence, it even shows from your facial expressions, speech, gestures, and behaviour patterns. An introspective analysis and improvement, as identified earlier, can help rectify that.
- Confidence is of two kinds: good confidence, and bad confidence. Good confidence is a positive feeling inside you that tells you that you know what you are doing, and you have the ability to accomplish whatever you want to. This is the mature and humble aspect of confidence. Bad confidence is arrogance - this is when you think you know everything, but at the same time you think that others don't know anything - that you are the only one who knows the ultimate truth. I call it - defying the laws of nature. Because, I believe that God, in his infinite wisdom, did two things: (a) gave everyone almost equal intelligence in their own areas of thought processes and capabilities, and (b) created everyone different, perhaps intentionally. So, all of us are equal as well as different, rather than better or worse. Each one of us have our own strengths and weaknesses, likes and dislikes.

- Arrogance is also, I think, the first sign of lack of confidence and maturity.
- Arrogance steps in when you think you know everything and you close your mind to further learning and different opinions and ideas. Learning is a never-ending process. When you stop learning, you will have the tendency to switch to opinions rather than facts. That is the beginning of bigotry, arrogance, and complacency. We live and learn by sharing throughout our lives. No one can be so boastful and presumptuous as to believe that he/she doesn't need to learn any more.
- Another important aspect of self-confidence is that you should always build your self-esteem and self-confidence on the strength of your own capabilities and achievements, rather than on the strength of others. Your own accolade, praise, and satisfaction is far more important than others. Enhance your self for your own self, not for others.
- Also, to grow big, you have to think big. When you think small, you remain small. So, you should not harbour on small, trivial, and meaningless achievements and petty deliberations of your day to day activities - you should develop a broader and mature outlook and perspective on activities.

8. COURAGE

- The key to success is to have the courage to stand out - to be different - to be positive - and to have self-confidence. Courage, coupled with passion and determination, is the most potent force that drives individuals towards excellence.
- Courage to operate with sincerity and freedom heightens self-confidence and self-esteem. In work situations, it is generally the fear of losing one's job that inhibits the drive for creativity and excellence. But really, when you think of it, losing your job has nothing to do with fear. You never lose your job just because you are afraid, or just because you are afraid would not protect you from losing your job. For, if you are to lose your job, you will lose it anyway. As a matter of fact, fear portrays lack of confidence. So, it is absolutely essential for personal success, to work with a free and open mind - to have self-confidence and courage to undertake responsibility to accomplish things.
- Finally, the last word of wisdom is "simplicity". Simplify your life. Many of us believe that good life and freedom is impossible without affluence, cut-throat competition, and conflict. The cultivation and expansion of needs is the antithesis of wisdom. Life based on "having" rather than "doing" or "being' breeds boredom, ennui, and a sense of isolation and soul-weariness. Simplicity is the key to freedom and fulfilment.

In attempting to summarize our message, the essentials of personal success can be encapsulated in the following three attributes:

- ▶ Confidence to stand up and be counted
- ▶ Courage to speak your mind
- ▶ Courage to be different
- ▶ Passion for whatever you do
- ▶ Passion for excellence and precision
- ▶ High entrepreneurial energy and enthusiasm
- ▶ High-level organizational ability
- ▶ Unflinching determination to achieve excellence

9

PERSONAL TQM

PERSONAL TQM: A CUT ABOVE

Personal TQM
(TQM: Total Quality Management)

Achieving self-discipline and personal
excellence through inner personal awakening.

Hopefully, we have created a "new person" in the previous chapter. We now wish to take this transformed person into the work environment, and identify the new roles and responsibilities for this new person towards personal and organizational success. The emphasis in this chapter is on the person - to exercise self-awakening - the awakening of the inner drive and passion to achieve excellence. We annotate it as Personal TQM.

Before we proceed, let us just recapitulate the intent of the thought processes discussed in the proceeding chapters:

▸ Business success is the primary aspiration of every enterprise.
▸ Success comes through doing consistently better and better than before in whatever you are doing.
▸ The main axle that drives every activity is the human individual.
▸ Success, therefore, depends on how energetic, dedicated, and productive the individual is.
▸ Individual's drive for excellence comes through his personal motivation.
▸ Motivation is something that resides and is generated within the individual.
▸ There are basically two ways of generating workforce motivation: management driven, and/or employee self-generated.

- ▸ Since motivation is a human-dependent phenomenon, nothing can happen unless the individual is willingly predisposed to being motivated.
- ▸ The major portion of our efforts should, therefore, be directed towards finding ways and means to help convince and strengthen an individual's psyche to inculcate a desire for self-discipline.
- ▸ Motivation is a direct consequence of a worker's attitude and state of happiness with the work environment.
- ▸ Since attitude determines motivational threshold, how can we induce a positive attitude and a performance mindset. There are, basically, two ways to accomplish this task:
  - • Management to provide: commitment, support, suitable working environment, transparency of operations, and genuine love and care for the workforce. This would be the subject of our discussion in the next few chapters.
  - • Employees to exercise: judicious cognitive appraisal of the environment around them; better self-control and self-discipline; greater sense of accountability, responsibility, and empathy towards the organization. This would be the mainframe of our discussion in this chapter.

With this synopsis, we shall now proceed to expound on our new Personal TQM concept to show how motivation can be generated by helping the individual to help himself in accepting greater sense of responsibility and challenge to develop greater self-discipline and high performance mindset.

The overall premise of the Personal TQM concept can be stated as follows:

- ▸ To urge the individual worker to inculcate a more realistic appreciation of the workplace predicaments.
- ▸ To prompt the worker to exercise better controls over his perceptual evaluation capabilities in order to make more judicious and unbiased decisions.
- ▸ To incite the worker to form a habit of being consistently positive in his attitude.
- ▸ To awaken the worker to accept greater sense of responsibility and accountability towards motivating himself.
- ▸ To guide the worker on how to develop self-discipline and total self-management.

Why do we need a new paradigm of motivation? As we have indicated earlier, business environment is flipping over so rapidly that the rules of business operability are being rewritten virtually everyday. Our thought processes, methods, and systems, therefore, also have to keep up the same pace in order to remain viable and meaningful. For tomorrow's workforce, the motivation methods of yesterday are not going to be workable. With new demands, we must think and act anew. We need a realignment of our old models and methods - the Personal TQM approach provides one such avenue for realignment. The strength and viability of this approach rests on the following premise:

> ► That, the old methods of motivating the workforce collectively as one whole unit are not going to be viable for the highly democratized workplace of the impending new millennium, in which people would be operating, more or less, as independent and self-reliant units. That, we need more self-driven and self-improving strategies that would be more compatible with the self-sufficiency of the new economic order.

> ► That, although management has an important role to play towards motivating the workforce, the workforce have an equal, if not greater, responsibility towards being self-motivated and self-disciplined.

> ► That, knowing the fact that every individual has an innate desire for excellence and fulfilment, we should utilize this handicap and attempt to go down to the root source of motivation - the human psyche - to evoke this desire and quest for excellence from within the individual - that is the basic premise of Personal TQM.

The Personal TQM concept is simply a re-enactment of an old thought, but with a new punch - and a very powerful one. It is about going deep down to tap the hidden reservoirs of dormant, but highly potent, energy and personal strength from within the individual. Personally I feel, that, when it comes to human motivation, we have been knocking on the wrong doors for a very long time - attempting to cure the symptoms rather than the disease - being overly preoccupied with developing and implementing rigidly structured and improperly focused motivation programs - being more worried about effective administration of the system logistics rather than concerned about the human element, which is the heart and soul of motivation - annotating management as the sole bearer of responsibility for generating and inducing motivation - shifting blames and responsibilities on each other when programs do not achieve the expected results - and living in quiet desperation over what to do with this dilemma of worker motivation. You know - we have to do none of the above - we simply have to put things in the right perspective - to understand what motivation really means - why it is important - what do we expect from a motivated person - where does motivation come from - who is responsible for generating motivation - how can we share the task and responsibility for rejuvenating the workplace - this is what we need to undertake slowly and systematically to handle the issue.

EMPLOYEE GRUMBLES: A HEALTHY DOSE OF REALITY

Remember, in the previous chapter, I outlined some corridor moans and groans of disgruntled employees. While there is validity in many of those lamentations and annoyances, there is always a possibility that these grievances may be the result of a worker's own faulty assumptions, selfish expectations, or misinterpretations of management's actions and intentions. And since we know that it is these negativistic aspects of a worker's perceptual framework that becomes an impediment in the way of motivation, I must bring some of these behavioural idiosyncrasies into the open to clear the air. It is imperative that I do that, because this is the first step to enacting Personal TQM - recognition of reality. The entire basis of Personal TQM hinges on the right perspective of a worker's attitude. Regretfully, my narrative is going to be bitterly, but realistically, candid - though, it is only meant to give a wake-up call to each worker to rise above the ordinary and imbibe a mature understanding of the uncial realities of operating a business.

Attitude formation is totally in the hands of an individual. A worker can waste his efforts and energies on negative brooding and self-degeneration, or he can choose to be more responsible in proactively sharing his concerns with the management to resolve issues amicably. Many workers shun establishing direct contact with the management. Instead, they let their cognitions formulate, in quiet desperation, incongruous opinions about management that, at times, are based totally on illustriously misleading expectations. This section is directly addressed to these people - it's an appeal to each worker to resort to a personal self-analysis to see how far it is their own idiosyncrasies or misconceptions, behavioural or otherwise, that may be responsible for their attitude towards the organization. Unless this is done, there would be little hope for achieving self-directed motivation. I would now outline some candid realities and I personally solicit and beseech to each of you to conscientiously contemplate on these aspects:

> ▸ Let's begin with your personal goals - and I hope you do have them. If your personal mission or agenda, whatever it may be - higher salary, rising up in the ranks, extra management responsibilities, etc. - is different or incompatible with that of the organization - you are in trouble. You have two choices - resolve this enigma with management or find another suitable place to work, that is compatible with your needs and expectations. If you don't do that - you will be constantly in conflict with either yourself or the organization. Either way, the point that I want to reinforce is that no organization will tolerate that a person whom they have hired and whom they are paying a salary, would be working against their own best interests. Remember, the organization is not

going to alter or change or realign its mission to make it compatible with that of each employee - employees have to work hard to operate within the framework of the organization's agenda. Indeed I do agree that management also has a responsibility to ensure that employees' goals and expectations are respected and fulfilled to the extent possible, and that an atmosphere of common understanding is created so that everyone can comfortably work under a shared vision.

▸ There is one indomitable fact that every individual worker must seriously keep in mind - that management has not hired you to create problems - they have hired you to solve problems, to help them, and to work with them in achieving the organization's goal.

▸ Try to understand that management has a different set of responsibilities and pressures than you do. They have to make the business a success, and for that they may have to take any number of drastic, but requisite measures. At the working level, it is sometimes difficult to fully comprehend the management's perspective or fully appreciate the judiciousness of their actions and decisions. But that is no reason why you should not join hands with management to try to assist them in their efforts to maintain the organization's agenda. Remember! management does not have all the answers - for if they did, they would not have hired you. They need your help - give it to them - proactively.

▸ There are some colleagues at the operational level who seem to be always insistently harbouring on that age old question: "what has management done for me - why should I do any more than what I am supposed to do". Let me make a plea to these friends - can you instead, ask the same question to yourself - what have you done for the management over and above the call of duty - over and above for what you have been paid for. Just try to go out of your way, at least once, and do something good for the management - and watch for the results. You will be pleasantly surprised that dedicated efforts, genuine help and support never goes unnoticed and unrewarded. People who willingly, proactively, and selflessly go out of their way to help management are the people who earn credibility, management trust, and ultimately higher ranks of responsibility.

▸ Let me address one of the worst scenarios - there are lots of workers who uphold the belief that their motivation and hard work should be compensated with suitable rewards, financial or otherwise. To some extent, I agree that these expectations are reasonable and that management should endeavour to recognize an employee's contribution and establish a suitable framework of opportunities for growth and development for every worker at every level of the organization. However, such demands become totally untenable when the worker's emotive responses try to establish a permanent one-to-one association between hard work and reward - that is, one happening only if the other happens - this I call "vocational blackmail".

There are two important messages that I wish to bring home from this type of faulty premonitions. First, no organization can afford to hand over financial rewards and/or promotions on a continual basis - it's just not possible. If an organization begins to intertwine job performance with incentives, it would very soon, either go out of business or be bankrupt. If a worker is rewarded for a particular job well done, what happens when the task is completed - the worker would either become less productive or get demoralized or he would work more harder so that he can produce some more better results against which he can ask for another reward. This is not how businesses can be run. Second, and more importantly, in today's business environment, the job that you have is, in itself, a reward. You are selected for the job and allowed to carry on in the job, with the underlying assumption that you are a self-starter, a self-motivated and a self-disciplined person. There is no understanding that you are to be given something extra, over and above the job that you have been given in order to be productive. Your job that you are taking for granted is your bonus and reward. You are supposed to be creating excellence at all times, as a normal routine process, and not whenever you are given additional incentives. And if you do not produce excellence at all times, that should be enough of a reason to terminate your appointment - there is no such thing as a lifetime job guarantee - at least not in today's volatile business environment.

From my own personal experiences, I have observed that this type of idiosyncratic misunderstanding is more prevalent among workers who have been in their jobs for a long time. Perhaps, this is so because they are the ones who feel trapped in positions which seemingly have no further opportunities for growth and development. Or perhaps, these people have become too comfortable in their jobs - they take the position as their given right - and they are now seeking for something extra - something over and above their present job which they consider as inherently theirs anyway.

▶ In the same token, if you say that you are doing your job satisfactorily as long as you are doing what you are being asked to do, then from my own personal perspective, I would say that you are really doing nothing. Because, by just doing what you are supposed to do, you are not doing any favour to anyone - you are being paid for that. The question to ask yourself is, "what I am doing over and above the call of duty for the organization". You have to assess for yourself if you are just a doer of things or an innovator - do you work in a reactive mode or proactive mode. In the reactive mode, the external motivators may be able to coerce you or force you to get motivated, but it wouldn't last for long. When you respond to situations proactively, and you voluntarily and willingly accept responsibility, you are well on your way to generating a self-directed sense of motivation and self-discipline that would be permanent and sustainable, and of which you would be truly proud of. Now a bit of healthy dose of reality for those people who practice the workplace ritual commonly known as : "look busy, do nothing". If you are the type who is always exuding the perception of being very busy, but in reality your total output is below the levels expected of a person with your knowledge and experience - watch out - there are always some mysterious forces at work that can single you out. Remember! Abraham Lincoln's saying - which is very true even to date - "you can befool some people all the time, all people some of the time, but you cannot befool all people all of the time". People with such work ethics never reach the higher levels of responsibility and success - or at least, if they did in the traditional work environment, they would not be able to do so in this new knowledge-based society, where tangible evidence of hard work is a minimum requirement for survival.

▸ Let's talk about the matter of self-deception - if you are wasting time at the workplace by doing chores that are unrelated to work-oriented performance, such as, playing the computer games, cruising through the Internet, working at the tasks slowly and unproductively, and you are happy that time passes by and also no one takes a notice of your idiosyncratic behaviour - beware - you are not wasting anyone else's time but your own - in fact, you don't waste time, time wastes you - you are simply deceiving your own self, and hurting yourself - you are making yourself redundant slowly and systematically - unconsciously you are cheating your own self.

Be vibrant and alive at the workplace - disseminate an aura of positive energy around you - proactively participate in all requisite activities - proactively accept challenges and responsibilities - be exuberant. Be alive and cognizant of what's happening in the company, and find out where and how you can help and make a contribution. Don't just wait until someone comes to ask you for your help - go out of your way to proactively offer help whenever you see it is needed. Everything that happens in the company is everyone's responsibility - share that responsibility equally and pleasantly.

▸ Lastly, let me interject a bit of my own personal perspective to work and life. If the entire purpose of your life is to be subservient to the routine: getting-up, going to work, doing what you are told, coming home - and the whole routine, all over again, day-in and day-out - that is totally demeaning and de-humanizing in my perspective. You have to do something invigorating each day, so that there is something new and challenging to look forward to each day. Even if you think that you don't want to or have to do it for the organization, you have at least to do it for yourself - you owe it to yourself, your own satisfaction - you have to fulfil yourself, if not anybody else. Getting home from work quickly or getting ahead at work quickly, whatever your passion, determines your motivation

Get-up - wake-up - rise above the ordinary - create - innovate - give your personal best and receive the best - you don't have to simply sit and wait for things to happen or circumstances to change - you have the power of the body, the mind, and the soul to make things happen - you are endowed with limitless source of strength and energy to create excellence, "if you want to" - do it.

I would now like to summarize the premise of my rather outspoken and frank narrative. Personal TQM can only be activated if we recognize the realities of the business world in their right perspective and make a concerted effort to generate self-discipline from within us through personal dedication and commitment. External forces do play a part in helping to augment the process, but there has to be a genuine inner desire to achieve one's personal best. This is the premise of Personal TQM. As a matter of fact, I would bluntly say that if an individual gets motivated only through the help of external pressures, or if he is addicted to unfulfilling routine work habits and has no desire to enhance his performance, then this paradigm is totally inept for such an individual.

But, having said that, my own personal convictions and experiences provide me with ample testimony, strength, and support to insistently assert that every individual human person has been endowed with this innate desire to excel. That, if this aspiration is seemingly dormant or does not properly manifest itself, it must be simply due to the influence of some prevailing circumstances under which the individual is operating and upon which he may not have any controls. It is my unflinching belief that human strength, endeavour, and will is always there - and it can create virtual miracles if it is properly channelled. It needs two-pronged impetus - the individual to wake-up from within to strive for excellence, and the management to endeavour to create an environment in which the worker can grow and succeed.

PERSONAL TQM: THE PROCESS

The process of Personal TQM starts with an introspective analysis, through which every individual identifies his strengths and weaknesses, his needs and requirements, and his personal contributions to the organization as well as the organization's contributions to the individual.

Before we begin the formal process of introspection, try this rather simple, but crude, introspective drill for a start. Pick up one typical day of your work life. At the end of the day, when you are returning home, driving your car, riding in a bus, or somnolently walking, ask yourself the question, "what did I do all day today".

- ▸ Seven telephone calls
- ▸ Four cups of coffee
- ▸ Five times to the washroom
- ▸ An hour for lunch
- ▸ A few chats with the colleagues in the corridors
- ▸ A few memos read, signed, or passed on.
- ▸ What else?

Sounds awfully funny - doesn't it? But, it is pretty astute to make a point. Ask yourself if you can tangibly and precisely identify what you accomplished during the whole day's work. Remember, no one is asking you this - it is you asking yourself. No one is even listening to what you are saying to yourself. This is not going to go into your performance appraisal or personnel file. You are the defendant, the prosecutor, the judge, and the jury - all in one. You are not being asked to be accountable to anyone but yourself. After all, for life to have any meaning, one has to be honest at least to oneself if not to anyone else.

Once you have identified your day's accomplishments, now ask yourself if that was adequate and satisfactory - was the day fulfilling or was it just another day, another dollar - thank God it's over - until tomorrow.

This is the beginning of Personal TQM - the start of a wave for self-awakening. From here on, we need to conduct a more formal and thorough introspective analysis. The following table presents a list of some probing questions that should form an integral part of the introspective analysis.

INTROSPECTIVE ANALYSIS: QUESTIONS

Vision/Mission

1. Do I have a personal vision?
2. Do I have personal short-term and long-term goals?
3. Do I know organization's mission, objectives, and goals?
4. Are my goals compatible with that of the organization?
5. How often have I discussed my needs and expectations with the management?
6. Is management receptive to my needs?

Roles/Responsibilities

7. Do I know the overall infrastructure of the organization?
8. Is the organization's operability transparent and open?
9. What is my role in the organization?
10. In what processes am I involved?
11. What is the extent of my responsibilities in the organization?
12. Have I been given adequate responsibilities?
13. Who is my inter/intra cross-functional interface?
14. Am I empowered?
15. Do I know my personal potentials?
16. Is management aware of my personal capabilities?
17. Is the management's perspective about my personal capabilities compatible with my own perception of my capabilities?
18. Is my role commensurate with my education, training, and experience?

Training/Development

19. Do I have adequate education, training, and experience to do my job.?
20. Have I been given appropriate training to do my job?
21. What training and development opportunities are available to me?

Attitude/Responsiveness

22. How is my attitude towards people?
23. What is other people's perception about my attitude?

INTROSPECTIVE ANALYSIS: QUESTIONS (CONT'D)

Attitude/Responsiveness (cont'd)

24. How helpful am I to others?
25. Do I operate in a positive or negative way?
26. Do I operate in a reactive or proactive manner?
27. How do I work in a team environment?
28. Do I actively and effectively participate in a team effort?
29. Do I proactively respond to challenges?
30. Do I willingly accept responsibility?

Self-Management/Self-Discipline

31. How do I handle change?
32. Do I manage my time well?
33. Am I limited to doing what someone tells me to do, or am I a self-motivated doer and innovator.
34. Do I take positive attitude during discussions?
35. Do I take control and ownership of processes in my own hands?
36. Am I receptive to suggestions?
37. How helpful am I to the management?
38. What do I do over and above the call of duty?
39. Am I doing my job productively?
40. At the end of the day, can I tangibly identify my accomplishments?

Job Satisfaction/Opportunities

41. Am I satisfied with the nature and level of my job?
42. Would I say that this is my dream job?
43. Am I fulfilled?
44. Have I ever analytically measured and evaluated my performance?
45. Is management sympathetic and helpful?
46. How is my rapport with management?
47. Do I have adequate opportunities for growth?

Contribution/Planning

48. How often do I do introspective analysis to evaluate my attitude and my performance?

INTROSPECTIVE ANALYSIS: QUESTIONS (CONT'D)

Contribution/Planning (cont'd)

49. Do I know my strengths and weaknesses?
50. Do I have a plan of action to eliminate or reduce my deficiencies?
51. Do I have a long-term plan to improve my performance?
52. What is my contribution to myself?
53. What is my contribution to the organization?
54. What is my contribution to society?

The set of questions appended in the above table represent only a sample of the concept of introspection analysis process. These queries can be further modified or augmented as per your own personal circumstances or workplace requirements. Once an individual has undergone an introspective analysis on these lines, he/she has to generate a framework for self-superimposing Personal TQM for achieving overall improvement and self-discipline. For this purpose, the sequence of steps outlined below can be followed.

The process outlined in the table below should generate ample information to proceed further for developing the following profile of the individual:

▸ Personal strengths and weaknesses
▸ Personal needs and requirements
▸ Nature and extent of organizational support required
▸ Basic framework for improvement

From here on, there is a need for joint effort between the management and the individual to evaluate the profile and take requisite action. The following action steps can be considered:

▸ Management evaluates the identified needs and requirements of the individual. These needs can be discussed on a one-to-one basis with the individuals or a combined profile of the common needs of individuals can be developed and discussed in a group meeting. The choice of these two options would, indeed, depend on the nature of needs. For example, some needs that are personal to each individual would have to be discussed on a one-to-one basis, while a common set of needs relating to the working environment and operability in general can be discussed in a group meeting.

INTROSPECTION ANALYSIS PROCESS

1. Introspection Analysis:
Identify your current state of functional performance.

2. Gap Analysis:
Identify your strengths and weaknesses.

3. Needs Analysis:
Identify what needs to be done to enhance your performance.

4. Action Analysis:
Develop a systematic approach to implement the planned set of activities.

5. Performance Analysis:
Evaluate the extent of improvements made.

6. Reinforcement Analysis:
Exercise continuous introspection, appraisal, and re-energization.

- ► Management identifies and provides requisite system support.
- ► The individual draws up a plan of action identifying how he/she will achieve:
  - Harmony with the management and the worklife
  - Job satisfaction and happiness
  - Self-discipline and optimum performance level

We shall expound further on the implementation and action plan in details in a later chapter. Now, in the remainder of this chapter, we shall elucidate some additional considerations pertaining to Personal TQM that are imperative for the effectuation of total self-management.

PERSONAL TQM: THE 7-ABSOLUTES

Motivation is an entity that drives individuals to achieve optimum levels of excellence and greater success in anything they do. Motivation begins with the individual and ends with the individual. Personal TQM is a harmonal therapy to achieve motivation - an emotional appeal to the psyche of the individual - to awaken, rekindle, and stimulate a sense of self-imposed accountability, regimentation, and a genuine desire to improve his performance, the resultant effect of which would be:

- ▸ Self-discipline, self-fulfilment, embellishment, and satisfaction
- ▸ Organizational growth and success
- ▸ Societal enrichment

What drives an individual to be motivated:

- ▸ His positive attitude
- ▸ His happiness and well-being at work
- ▸ His harmony with the management and the work environment
- ▸ His control over events that transpire in his personal and work life

With this frame of mind, we would now proceed to outline the "*Personal TQM Absolutes*", appended below, required to inculcate and evolve a total rejuvenation of the personal self. The axioms are followed by explanatory discussion which, we hope, would provide sufficient ammunition for any individual worker, in any situation and circumstance, to generate a self-directed motivation drive and to enlighten his modus operandi to achieve higher realms of excellence.

PERSONAL TQM
The 7-Absolutes
P-1: Create a personal vision
P-2: Determine personal potential
P-3: Practice proactive participation
P-4: Develop performance mindset
P-5: Exercise self-discipline
P-6: Develop empathy for the organization
P-7: Exercise continual self-analysis

P-1: CREATE A PERSONAL VISION

- ▸ It is absolutely important to have a purpose in life. A purposeless life is totally demeaning and dehumanizing.
- ▸ Set a personal vision for yourself. Since a vision is an outcome of a desire, it keeps you alive and rejuvenated. You look forward for something invigorating each day. You cannot simply go to work each day just to earn money,

howsoever important and requisite it may be - there has to be something more than that - your personal satisfaction and pride in what you do - your personal enjoyment and fulfilment - a sense of achievement - a sense of victory.

▸ Set goals for yourself - short-term as well as long-term. Unless you have a set of well-defined goals, you won't be able to validate your achievements, contributions, the organization's input towards you, and your overall level of performance and fulfilment.

▸ Make sure that your goals are compatible with your overall profile - education, training, experience, potentials and capabilities. If this is not so, you will be constantly in conflict with yourself.

▸ Your mission must be commensurate with the organization's mission. If it is not so, there would be continuous tension at the workplace and this can influence the self-directed motivational efforts. Firstly, indeed, it is the organization's responsibility to ensure that a common shared vision is effectively communicated to all employees at all levels of the organization. However, remember that it is not the organization's responsibility to align its goals with that of every employees' - it is your responsibility to ensure that your expectations and goals are compatible with that of the organization. If they are not, then you should proactively discuss them with your managers to strike a balance and harmony. It is only when you are working toward a shared vision that you will enjoy peer support, organizational sustenance, and personal mental peace, satisfaction, and fulfilment.

P-2: DETERMINE PERSONAL POTENTIAL

▸ You must have a clear understanding of the nature and extent of your roles and responsibilities, and how and where they fit in the overall framework of the organization. This is important for three reasons: for you to be working in positions that are commensurate with your potentials; for you to be intrinsically satisfied with your roles and responsibilities; and for you to derive a feeling of satisfaction that your input is making a meaningful contribution to yourself and to the organization.

▸ Until and unless you and the management clearly understand the scope of your personal role, you cannot expect to initiate personal improvement impetus. Your work assignments must be regularly discussed with the management to ensure that your potentials are optimally utilized.

▸ When you are intrinsically satisfied with your personal role, you will automatically exude a positive attitude towards work and getting motivated would be relatively easy.

- It is important to have a feeling of belonging in order to be happy and motivated. You cannot just go to work day in and day out, do what you are told, and still uphold the feeling that you are making a meaningful contribution.
- It is also very important to ensure that there is minimal differential between management's perception of your capabilities and your own perception about your potentials. A large majority of the time, employees have been found to be disgruntled on the premise that management have by-passed them in favour of other employees, and have not given them the opportunity for higher responsibility or better status that they really deserve by virtue of their capabilities. This has been observed to be a major source of low morale and low productivity. Remember! There is always the possibility that what you think about yourself and your potentials is not the same as what management thinks about it. Work positively and maturely over this issue and resolve the dilemma, if it exists, with the management. Either demonstrate to the management that you have greater potential for higher responsibilities, or systematically assess your strengths and weaknesses through introspective analysis and work towards improving your capabilities.
- Once you understand what your roles and responsibilities are, try to assess, as effectively as possible, your potentials and capabilities. This is important for two reasons: for you and the management to know what capabilities you have so that you can be assigned to appropriate work assignments; and to help identify your training and development needs.
- A knowledge of your personal potentials would also help you to:
  - Set realistic goals and expectations
  - Consider possibilities of multiple work assignments
  - Seek appropriate opportunities for growth and development
  - Realize job satisfaction and self-fulfilment
- Personal TQM puts emphasis on you - to know your strengths and weaknesses, to identify your current best, and to proactively seek avenues and opportunities for improvement. Unless you and the management have a clear idea about your potentials and capabilities, you cannot expect to realize your goals.

P-3: PRACTICE PROACTIVE PARTICIPATION

- Work in a proactive rather than reactive mode. Go out of your way to respond to challenges and accept responsibility. Don't wait for people to come and ask you for your help - be proactive in finding out where and how you can help - everyone in the organization has equal responsibility towards fulfilling the organization's mandate.

- Actively and willingly participate in team efforts. This is a world of interactive systems - interdependence is an integral part of today's business operability. We live and learn by sharing. Sharing provides us with enormous pleasure, dividends, and opportunities for growth.
- Try to inculcate a positive outlook in teamwork. Argue, discuss, criticize, but provide positive ideas and solutions. Be a problem solver not a problem creator.
- Work and grow under the participatory umbrella of a shared vision. The organization depends on you to provide support and cooperation. Help develop a supportive and vibrant culture. Grow in togetherness.

P-4: DEVELOP PERFORMANCE MINDSET

- To achieve excellence and success, you must believe in excellence - which means working conscientiously at a high performance level at all times. Performance mindset is achieved through personal dedication, continuous reinforcement, and trust in yourself.
- Don't just be a doer of things - be creative and innovative. Keenly study the processes that you are involved in and try to think of new and better ways of doing things. If you are only doing what you are told to do, you are wasting a precious commodity - your potential. Improvements don't just happen - they are caused by innovative people. There is always a sense of pride in creativity - it's yours for the asking. Envious levels of success can only be achieved through envious levels of dedication and performance.
- Do not waste your energies by harbouring on the negative feelings that management doesn't listen to you - you do your personal best anyway - good ideas would never go unheeded and wasted. Don't keep good ideas inside you, share them with your peers and superiors - it needs only one good idea to create a miracle - the miracle of success.

P-5: EXERCISE SELF-DISCIPLINE

- Positive attitude is the foremost precursor to motivation. It is the single most important factor that influences your motivation threshold. A person with a positive attitude is a happy worker - he radiates positiveness and affability all around him. A person with a negative attitude generally expends much of his efforts and energies fighting with the system or grappling with his own unfulfilled expectations.
- Attitude is an entity that resides within the individual. It is formulated by the individual internally through his own thought processes. The individual

perceives external circumstances, evaluates their viability against his own beliefs and expectations, and makes a judgemental value for their acceptance or rejection. If the external conditions are acceptable, the person would display harmony with the system and be conducive to being motivated. If there is a conflict between what he perceives and what he expects, he would be more occupied in resolving this conflict rather than concerned about motivation. The evaluative function is undertaken by the person's cognitive faculties, and the results of the evaluation are stored into his limbic system as emotive reactions and attitudes. Therefore, to generate a positive attitude, the individual must do the following:

- Endeavour to obtain reliable information from management concerning the issue in question.
- Endeavour to make unbiased and judicious cognitive evaluations of the situation.
- Continually evaluate the degree of congruence between his emotive reactions and his work environment.
- Practice to maintain a healthy and happy attitude at all times.
- Exercise self-discipline and self-control. To create harmony at the workplace, you must control your attitude, behaviour, interactive response.
- The management also has a very important responsibility in this regard - to ensure that there is operational transparency and that the individual is continually provided with proper and sufficient information about the conditions that affect his work and performance.

P-6: DEVELOP EMPATHY FOR THE ORGANIZATION

- ➤ The first basic principle of human business management is mutual empathy - the worker for the organization and the organization for the worker. Empathy is a two-way street.
- ➤ If you don't have feelings for the welfare of the organization, how can you expect management to have feelings for your happiness and growth.
- ➤ Think it this way at least - the organization is providing you with sustenance - food on your table and a roof over your head - so, you owe it to the organization to give your honest personal best - to be genuinely concerned about the organization's success.
- ➤ The best way to accomplish this is to consider yourself the owner of the company - the chief executive officer - and, now it becomes your responsibility to look after the organization.
- ➤ Finally, if nothing else, you can consider empathy as a means to your own personal growth. Because, when you show concern for the organization and

you substantiate it with good performance and dedication, the management will undoubtedly take note of it, and reward you for your deeds in one form or another. Genuine efforts never go unnoticed or wasted.

P-7: EXERCISE CONTINUAL SELF-ANALYSIS

- Every once in a while, spend some time to self-assess your overall direction: what were your goals; what did you do to achieve those goals; how successful were you in your efforts; can you tangibly identify the extent of improvements made; what new steps are you contemplating taking to further improve your performance.
- Assess what significant contributions you are making towards the achievement of personal goals as well as organizational mandate.
- Routinely assess your personal fulfilment level.
- Personal TQM is a process of "continuous personal re-engineering". You must continuously undergo introspective analysis and draw upon your inner resources to: identify your strengths and weaknesses, assess your needs and requirements, develop a plan of action to improve your process performance, evaluate improvements made, and continue this cycle of Personal TQM process.

PERSONAL TQM SYNOPSIS

How would you rate yourself? Are you happy with your work life? Are you fulfilled? Do you display a pleasant attitude at work? Do people like you? Do you like people? Are you helpful to others? Do you accept responsibilities proactively and willingly? Do you enjoy your work? Do you make conscientious personal efforts to improve your productivity and performance.

If the answer to the above is "yes" - you are the sunshine of the world - you are the reason for the success of the organizations - you are a self-motivator and optimist of the business world.

If the answer is "no" - what's the matter - what's holding you back? Are you burned-out, stressed-out, confused, demoralized, or demotivated? If you are, is it because of the circumstances and conditions at the workplace under which you have to operate or is it because of your own internal conflicts and lack of harmony.

If it is the working environment that is causing you distress and aggravation, then you have to do something about it positively. You cannot simply continue living in quiet desperation and keep sulking about the situation. The situation cannot get resolved by itself. A good starting point would be to make a checklist - identify all aspects of work life that are incongruent to your personal expectations. Carry out an unbiased evaluation of your concerns and validate their judiciousness and efficacy. Now, try to develop a dialogue with your supervisor and discuss, in a positive manner, all of your concerns and feelings. Constantly work with the management and develop a harmony with the environment. Stress your opinions and desires as genuinely as possible, but always appreciate the management's predicaments, limitations, needs, and priorities. A positive resolve to the dilemma is bound to emerge out of your continuous positive collaboration with the management.

If, on the other hand, your uneasiness and malaise is due to a vague sense of inner dissatisfaction with your accomplishments, then you should know that this is a perfectly normal part of human thought processes. Temporary obstacles and setbacks do generate a feeling of failure every now and then. But, there is no need to get upset or depressed about these intermittent occurrences. Because, the power source of energy and potential is still within your control - you have the strength, the gut, and the capability to alter things and situations the way you want. What is more important is to keep your chin up and think positive. For example, think of obstacles as challenges and failures as learning experiences. Your own skills, intellect, and dedication are the real catalysts for success. So keep working on yourself - your abilities and strengths. And keep the motivational tempo on a continuum - because messages have short shelf life and they keep fading away quickly - so keep reinforcing your determination continuously. This is your game - you have to play it and play it well - you owe it to yourself.

10

THE MAKING OF A MANAGER

THE MANAGEMENT DILEMMA

Of all the grumbles and lamentations that we hear at the workplace about human resource, the following two complaints seem to be the most common:

- From the managers, we hear: we can't find good people - people who can think on their feet, without supervision or without constantly telling them what they have to do - people with initiative and drive - people who have a sense of responsibility and discipline - people with balanced skills, who have technological knowledge, as well as a caring attitude.
- From senior managers and executives we hear: we can't find good managers - managers who have the ability to provide effective leadership - who have the energy and charisma to motivate and drive people towards greater productivity and excellence.

Firstly, these enigmas have the same general answer: people are people - good people, whether workers or managers, don't grow out of the ground, or fall from heaven - you cannot find ready-made, prefabricated good people or managers - they have to be created through dedicated efforts. Secondly, we have to know how to build an efficient person - how to enhance a person's personality, outlook, efficiency, and self-management abilities to make him a good person - a good worker - and a good manager. In the preceding chapters, we have outlined extensive guidelines for realigning and augmenting an individual's personal awareness and growth in order to achieve self-discipline. Now, in this chapter, we shall present some new thoughts and ideas on how to build a good manager.

There are basically two options available to an organization to have good managers:

- Select people from the open market, who have proven track records as good managers. This option is weak, time-consuming, and expensive.

- Identify management potential from within the organization, and groom them to take a management position. This is the preferred option, which we are going to explore in this chapter.

The option of identifying people from within the organization and preparing them for greater responsibility is a very worthwhile undertaking, because of the following reasons:

- It establishes a "culture of caring" for the organization.
- It is very cost effective.
- It involves people who are already well versant with the organization's operational framework - consequently, they don't need to be trained as extensively as would have to be the case for someone totally new coming from the outside. This affords a good saving of time, as well as resolves any urgency problems for the organization.
- It helps to improve the overall morale at the workplace.
- It generates a healthy and positive internal competition among workers - to work hard, improve productivity, and prove their capability for advancement.

With this premise, we now wish to address the following critical questions:

- What are the characteristics of a good manager?
- How do we identify the management potential?
- How do we groom people for management positions?

BASIC QUALITIES OF A MANAGER

The most basic attributes of a good manager can be stated as follows. A good manager:

- Possesses high level organizational capability
- Has passion for precision
- Has enormous energy and enthusiasm
- Has obsession for performance and excellence
- Has good leadership abilities
- Has the ability to handle diverse situations, without being stressed
- Has the ability to handle multi-dimensional tasks with promptness and efficiency
- Has the courage to take risks
- Has confidence to make decisions
- Has a stable and mature personality

- Has a positive outlook and attitude towards everything
- Is judicious in his dealings
- Earns his respect not through the fear of his position and authority, but through the strength of his capabilities

IDENTIFYING MANAGEMENT POTENTIAL

It is not very difficult for management to identify people in the organization who can possibly be considered for management positions, if they take time to carefully analyse and evaluate the available knowledge about the individuals. In most organizations, we believe that, in general terms, everybody knows everybody else to some extent in varying degrees, depending on their working relation proximity. We all have that sixth sense to assess and evaluate people and draw-up a profile about the person. For example, in any workplace, people at large know: who is a good person; who is highly capable and skilled; who works very hard; who is honest; who is liked by everyone; etc. It is a common knowledge - a matter of common sense - a sense common to us all - to know the overall personality framework of each other.

The management can utilize information from the following sources to develop a profile of the possible potential management candidates:

- Employee's performance appraisal results
- Recommendations of section heads and managers
- Persons who have won company's awards and recognition for excellence, higher productivity, congeniality, innovativeness, suggestion of the year, or any other similar achievement award
- Records of achievement of other skills, education, training, or experience gained by the employee
- Records of participation by the individual in other activities of the organization leading to tangible or intangible benefits for the organization
- Records of innovative ideas and suggestions made by the employee in the past
- A general knowledge of person's likeability by other employees
- Results of a battery of tests that can be conducted on the individual for this specific purpose of identifying management skills

To gain credible information about an individual's management potentials, management should formalize the process. A well planned systematic set of procedures should be developed that would entail into forming a formal profile for each potential candidate.

In addition to the above process, which in itself is very useful and important, we are adding some new concepts in the equation. We believe that, the personality characteristics of a person bear the most profound influence on a person's operability framework - and hence, an evaluation of the person's personality should become an integral part of this selection process. For after all, we are looking for a strong management potential and capability, and not only a good person, or innovative person, or hard working person only.

The question is - which personality traits to consider? The complexity of the human person is virtually astronomical - there are numerous personality traits that, in lesser or greater degree, collectively influence the behaviour patterns of an individual. Given the enormity of the situation, we have come up with the following three factors, which we think bear the most influence, especially in the context of management capabilities: Aggressiveness, Maturity, Knowledge.

What we shall do now is to first elucidate our understanding of the meaning of these three factors. Then, we shall look at their correlational impact on a person's operability framework. Finally, we shall provide guidelines on how senior managers can utilize this personality aspect knowledge to select suitable management candidates and prepare and groom them for positions of increasing responsibility.

THE PERSONALITY FACTOR

Let us closely examine the impact of the three personality traits - aggressiveness, maturity, knowledge - on an individual's behaviour.

AGGRESSIVENESS

This characteristic has two aspects: good aggressiveness and bad aggressiveness. For a good manager, it is the good aggressiveness we need. *Good aggressiveness*, as per our connotation, means: drive, zeal, energy, that burning passion inside a person to be the best. *Bad aggressiveness* means: pushy, hostile, militant, repulsive, and downright obnoxious.

MATURITY

Means: motivation, fullness, stability, humility, wisdom, etc.

KNOWLEDGE

Means: education, training, experience, skills, intelligence, ability, judgement, comprehension, etc.

The real challenge for the upper management lies in the following:

- How to evaluate these characteristics?
- How to evaluate the level of each characteristic?
- How to estimate the right mix of the levels of these three characteristics for a good manager?

The evaluation of these three characteristics is by no means an easy task. The following three types of initiatives need to be effectuated for this:

- Some type of battery of tests to assess a person's level of aggressiveness (good aggressiveness), maturity, and knowledge.
- Through basic human instinct and evaluation capability.
- Through various work-related records, as indicated earlier.

Let me outline some naively simple intuitive guidelines for assessing a person's level on these three characteristics:

AGGRESSIVENESS

Generally speaking, aggressiveness can be assessed visually by looking at a person's eyes and the areas immediately around the eyes. Eyes are a window to a person's personality. Sharp, piercing, focussed, attentive, and searching eyes are normally associated with a person who has a passion and drive for knowing everything and wanting to achieve the ultimate success. The force with which a person speaks, his bodily gestures, his proactive behaviour patterns - all of these point to an aggressive personality. Of course, it is not to mean that persons with soft and unaggressive eyes or persons who do not display these characteristics are by any mean weaker in any sense of the term, or that they do not possess the energy and drive to accomplish things.

MATURITY

A visual estimation of a person's maturity level can be made from the way a person behaves: his manner of speech; his patience; ability to listen patiently to others; his positive outlook and attitude; stability; thoughtfulness in the way he asks or answers questions; judiciousness of his decisions, etc.

KNOWLEDGE

This characteristic, being technical in nature, can be easily estimated from the person's achievements: education, training, skills, experience, etc. In addition, this can also be viably evaluated through a battery of test.

THE MAKING OF A MANAGER

How can we use the knowledge of these three personality factors of a person to identify and develop a manager. To be able to do that, we need to establish a person's positioning of levels in relation to these characteristics - we are suggesting a grid-type analysis, as schematically shown below:

	Aggressiveness	Maturity	Knowledge
High (H)			
Medium (M)			
Low (L)			

What we need to do is to decipher a person's level of aggressiveness, maturity, and knowledge in terms of high, medium, and low gradations, and then develop the right mix requisite to becoming a manager. This aspect can be better elucidated and understood through the following examples:

Aggressiveness = H; Maturity = L; Knowledge = L

A person with this mix is a poor candidate for management positions or situations requiring leading people through teamwork.

Aggressiveness = H; Maturity = L; Knowledge = M/H

These are the typical characteristics of a high-powered, aggressive salesperson, who achieves good success for himself/herself as well as for the organization. A good salesperson would not necessarily be able to become a good manager without enhancing his/her maturity level.

Aggressiveness = L; Maturity = M; Knowledge = H

Typically, a high-skilled professional scientist, this person commands great respect among his peers, but lacks the aggressive drive to achieve higher levels of management.

Aggressiveness = L; Maturity = H; Knowledge = L/M

This person is a mentor to everybody, but lacks the passion required for managing people.

This is just a few examples of how grid analysis can be carried out to assess the mix of levels of a person's personality characteristics for suitability to managerial positions. This narrative is, by means, a gauge to measure the right or the wrong, the good or the bad - it is simply an observational device for establishing a viable profile for the individual. I believe that most people have this analytical capability - and if used in the right perspective, it can serve a very useful purpose for personality assessment.

In line with this method of evaluation, we would say that the following combination would generate the right mix for a "good manager":

- ▸ high aggressiveness
- ▸ high maturity
- ▸ medium to high levels of multi-dimensional knowledge

We shall now elucidate another new idea on how optimal job-personality compatibility can be achieved. This requires going back to the basic human functional entities:

- ▸ the brain
- ▸ the mouth
- ▸ the hands

Some people are good with their brain capabilities. They are more of thinkers than others. Such people are ideal for situations involving: research, analysis, designing, planning, strategic management, analytical evaluation, etc.

Others are good with the use of their mouth. These are people who are very well spoken, and have a good command of speech. People like these are very well suited to service-oriented areas, as spokespersons for the organization, as resource for training, etc.

Finally, people who are good with their hands are the highly skilled craftsmen, who are excellent in producing quality output.

The management's ingenuity lies in combining these three aspects of human functional entities, with the three personality characteristics of aggressiveness, maturity, and knowledge, and evolve a perfect combination by which an individual's capabilities can be used to its maximum. This optimal utilization can be achieved through optimal allocation of persons to the appropriate jobs. Initiatives that are conducive to such arrangements include: job rotation, job redesign, etc. We shall provide further details on this issue in a later chapter.

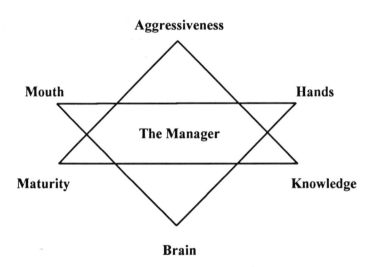

SYPNOSIS

The main premise of our discussion in this chapter is to reassert the fact that the management doesn't have to go out to search for good managers - they simply need to look inside the organization - and identify management potential that can be groomed and prepared for greater management responsibilities. Even personality readjustments can be effectuated, if needed, through effective training and coaching.

The important thing is to make sure that a persons' capability and personality characteristics are aptly matched with the nature of work, to achieve optimum levels of efficiency.

To recapitulate, we present here the grand list of qualities requisite to being a good manager:

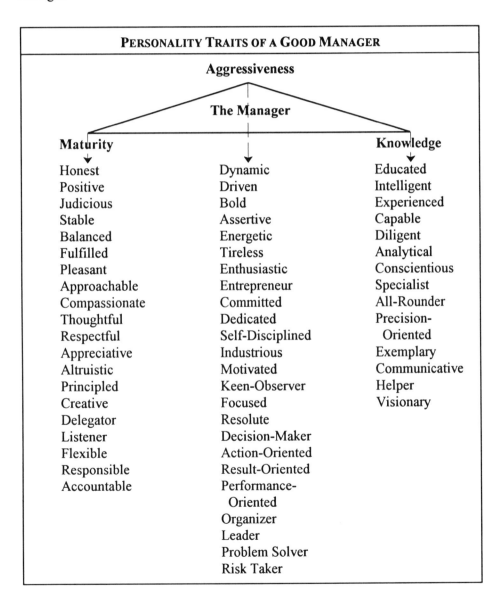

PERSONALITY TRAITS OF A GOOD MANAGER

Aggressiveness

The Manager

Maturity		Knowledge
Honest	Dynamic	Educated
Positive	Driven	Intelligent
Judicious	Bold	Experienced
Stable	Assertive	Capable
Balanced	Energetic	Diligent
Fulfilled	Tireless	Analytical
Pleasant	Enthusiastic	Conscientious
Approachable	Entrepreneur	Specialist
Compassionate	Committed	All-Rounder
Thoughtful	Dedicated	Precision-
Respectful	Self-Disciplined	Oriented
Appreciative	Industrious	Exemplary
Altruistic	Motivated	Communicative
Principled	Keen-Observer	Helper
Creative	Focused	Visionary
Delegator	Resolute	
Listener	Decision-Maker	
Flexible	Action-Oriented	
Responsible	Result-Oriented	
Accountable	Performance-	
	Oriented	
	Organizer	
	Leader	
	Problem Solver	
	Risk Taker	

Summarizing the above list, the most credible qualities of a good manager can be succinctly stated as follows:

A good manager:

- Always operates through a well defined purpose, goal, and agenda.
- Is totally committed and dedicated to the cause of the organization.
- Is well organized in his day-to-day activities as well as short-term and long-term priorities.
- Gets things done efficiently and with optimal precision.
- Has a passion for exactness, precision, and performance.
- Solves problems, not creates them.
- Knows how to manage teams for optimum results.
- Knows when and how to delegate.
- Is enthusiastic as well as infuses enthusiasm in his staff.
- Has the ability and strength to make on the spot, but judicious decisions.
- Has the drive to take initiatives.
- Is always full of positive energy.
- Has sufficient knowledge of all the processes.
- Has the ability to handle diverse situations.
- Can handle many things at the same time without being stressed.
- Continually seeks to improve processes.
- Treats everyone equally and fairly.
- Is always approachable.
- Is a good listener.
- Continually seeks his staff's opinion.
- Provides effective, timely, and positive feedback.
- Has compassion for his staff.
- Goes out of his way to thank and praise his staff's accomplishments.

11

MANAGEMENT TQM

MOTIVATION: A JOINT VENTURE

As indicated in our previous discussion, there are basically two main drivers of workforce motivation: the management, and the workers themselves. The preceding chapters were devoted to the necessity, importance and responsibilities of the individual workers to inculcate self-discipline through self-motivation. It was argued that motivational efforts of any type and magnitude would only yield tangible results when the individual worker is susceptible to being motivated and willingly exercises self-discipline. The argument we presented was a digression from the traditional way of thinking about motivation - we termed it as a new paradigm of "Personal TQM".

In this chapter, we shall deal with the other important aspect - the role of management in inducing motivation and rejuvenation in the workplace. While it is true that no amount of management convincing or coercing can invoke motivation among workers, unless the workers themselves accept this responsibility, it is also equally true that without the management's total commitment and dedicated participation, no motivational program can succeed. We are taking a fresh look at what management must do in this new economic age, against what they have been doing before, to enhance worker motivation and augment productivity levels. Once again we are digressing from the conventional wisdom and traditional modus operandi, and outlining a new paradigm shift for the role of management towards workforce motivation. To be consistent and in line with my previous phraseology, we are annotating this as "Management TQM (Total Quality Management)". In presenting our new approach and thoughts, we may have to be a bit hard on the management in identifying their deficiencies and idiosyncrasies. Unfortunately, we have to do that in order to suggest a healthy realignment of the management's roles and responsibilities for achieving better results.

MANAGEMENT'S IDIOSYNCRASIES: A HEALTHY SATIRE

The management is generally responsible for establishing the organization's mission, setting the ground rules for the functioning of the organization, and establishing a suitable framework and environment in which people can happily work and strive towards the fulfilment of the common shared vision. The workers, on the other hand, have the responsibility to perform their duties and functions in the most productive manner. Both parties have an equal role to play in motivating the workplace. Managers must endeavour to provide all requisite facilities to employees and follow good management principles to motivate and encourage people towards optimum performance. The employees must offer their genuine support, dedication, and commitment for the welfare of the organization.

Where and how the management fails in their efforts to motivate people - this is what we are going to discuss in this section? Once again like the last chapter, my narrative is going to impart a rather candid manifestation of our system management deficiencies. It is hoped that this information would provide a positive feedback for building more effective management strategies for the future.

It has been observed from experience that while management certainly helps to put a system in place, they do very little towards providing continuous leadership and support for system sustainability and success. Having implemented the motivational program, most managers side-step into their own ivory tower busyness, and expect that the program will go on without any further attention, input, and support from them.

Motivation is not like a piece of equipment or machinery that you install and assume that it will run smoothly forever without any attention. Motivation is a human-dependent phenomenon - it's memory span is very short - the message fades away quickly - you have to continuously reinforce the message. Motivation program, therefore, requires a continuous hands-on participation and exemplary leadership from the management.

The next idiosyncrasy pertains to the perception of roles and responsibilities for motivation. Most managers believe that having implemented the motivation program, their responsibility ceases and that it is now totally the worker's responsibility to motivate themselves. The irony of the dilemma is that the workers, on the other hand, uphold a complete reversal of this conjecture - they hold management to be the sole bearer of responsibility for inducing motivation. As a consequence, when the programs do not progress as smoothly and effectively as anticipated or envisaged by the management, they start blaming the workers. Managers keep on harbouring on the age-old excuse that the program is not achieving sustainable levels of success because the workers are not motivated.

It is imperative to understand that system success is a shared responsibility and all parties have to collectively work hard for it. Managers cannot possibly expect miracles to happen without making a significant contribution to the cause. Also, successes and failures have to be equally shared by all parties. Managers cannot just take the credit for putting the system in place or for its success, and shift the blame onto the workers when the system fails. Each party has equal contribution and accountability to both the successes as well as the failures.

Finally, shifting of responsibility and blame onto the workers may be genuine and acceptable as long as the managers can unquestionably validate that they have done their virtual best in providing all the requisite support and personal input into the process. To this end, I am appending below some soul-searching questions that I would like every manager to contemplate upon. The purpose of this introspective drill is to provide a wake-up call to the management - to assess for themselves the true viability and extent of their contribution to the cause, that is fundamental to the success of the program.

INTROSPECTIVE DRILL FOR MANAGEMENT

Contemplate on the following:

- What have I done over and above the call of duty to motivate my staff?
- Have I been personally involved with my employees at a hands-on operational level?
- Do I clearly understand the nature and magnitude of the job that the employees are expected to do - from my own, as well as, from the perspective of the workers?
- Do I know my employees' needs and requirements: operational, functional, and personal?
- Do I know the strengths and weaknesses of my staff?
- Do I have an estimate of the overall capacity and capability of my workers?
- Do I have any idea about the current productivity level of my staff?
- Do I know what is the optimum level of a particular job?
- Have I communicated the organization's mission to my staff in a clear manner?
- Have I provided clear directions to my staff?
- Have I shown exemplary leadership?
- Have I provided appropriate resources, tools, and support systems.
- Have I provided appropriate opportunities for training and development?
- What opportunities for improvement and growth have we provided?
- Have I empowered people to manage their processes?

- ► Do I have complete trust and confidence in my people?
- ► How often have I asked for my staff's opinion?
- ► How often have I recognized and credited my staff's contribution and dedication?

This is just a sample of some thought-provoking questions that you, as managers, should contemplate upon. Your answers to these questions would provide you with the awareness of the extent of your real and tangible contribution to the process of motivation. Motivation would never come by without your help. You cannot just sit and sulk over workers not endeavouring to motivate themselves. As a manager, you have tremendous responsibility on your shoulders to proactively immerse yourself into the process and provide effective leadership and direction. You have been chosen, over and above all other employees, to be the manager - that's what you should do - to manage - to provide hands-on input - to be proactive - to be mature, compassionate, and understanding - to utilize your management skills to solve problems, resolve issues, and seek viable solutions. You are expected to be a self-starter, a self-motivator - for if you cannot motivate yourself, how can you expect to motivate others or how can you expect others to self-motivate themselves - you have to take the initiative - you are the "manager".

MANAGEMENT TQM: THE 7-OBLIGATIONS

In line with the above discussion, we now present some valuable guidelines that managers can gainfully utilize for maintaining a continuous rejuvenation and re-energization of the workplace. The following table presents the "*Seven Management Obligations*", followed by some explanatory notes. These obligations are fundamental to the success of any motivation program.

MANAGEMENT TQM
The 7-Obligations
M-1: Give them purpose
M-2: Give them leadership
M-3: Give them information
M-4: Give them support
M-5: Give them ownership
M-6: Give them opportunity
M-7: Give them credit

M-1: GIVE THEM PURPOSE

- Let's begin with the question - "why should a worker get motivated"? There has to be a viable reason for that. Everything in life we do is because of a reason, a purpose. Life is meaningless without a purpose.
- Workers need to maintain a one-to-one correspondence between the purpose and action in order to be in a state of continual motivation. People feel happy, motivated, and willing to work towards the purpose - they get a sense of belonging - a sense of victory and pride in associating their action with the accomplishment of the purpose. No one likes to expend his energies towards a purposeless vacuum.
- It doesn't take long to explain to your employees the purpose of their undertaking. Give people the purpose of their work and watch them create miracles for you. Contemplate on the following - what I call the 11th commandment:

11TH MOTIVATIONAL COMMANDMENT

People are willing to perform any task once:

- They know why they are doing it
- They know what they will get out of it

- Since the purpose and mission is generally established by the management group, it is imperative that this be effectively communicated to all workers at all levels of the organization. Everyone must be collectively working towards a common vision.
- A purpose is a multi-layered entity - there is a purpose at every level of the organization that is commensurate with the operational and functional needs of that level. Also, purposes at various levels must always be interactive and intertwined. Each smaller purpose must serve another larger purpose. For example, every organization has a larger mission: success and profitability. This larger purpose is then accommodated by many smaller purposes of various dimensions, such as: productivity improvement, process control, production control, worker motivation, cost control, etc. All smaller purposes must collectively satisfy the intent of the larger purpose.
- Finally, let me give you a real life example to illustrate the importance of purpose and its impact on motivation. While consulting for a large

manufacturing company, one day I stopped in the plant and asked a worker who was collecting process control data and measurements, "why are you gathering this data". Hesitantly, but truthfully, the person replied, "I don't really know why I am doing it and what purpose it is supposed to serve - nobody tells me what it is for - nobody even uses this information - I just keep doing what I am asked to do." Can you imagine what kind of motivation can be expected from a person who has never been told the purpose of his work?

M-2: GIVE THEM LEADERSHIP

▸ Management participation, direction, and leadership plays a vital role in the process of motivation. Motivation programs cannot achieve their intended goals without a continuous interplay of actions between the management and the workers. It is in the inherent nature of every work environment that employees are always looking for good management support and leadership - leadership that is trustworthy, provides clear sense of direction, and assists the employees in improving their performance.

▸ Most importantly, employees value exemplary leadership - leaders who can lead by example. Unfortunately, you can still find scores of managers in every organization who still strongly uphold the out-dated premise that managers are only supposed to show the way but not tread the path with the workers. To some managers, especially those who have been in the management positions for a reasonably long time, managing only means telling others what to do but not doing it yourself. If you cannot do what you say, you cannot expect others to do anything, at least willingly. As managers, you may have the power to coerce or force others to do things that you don't do yourself, but it cannot last for long. This holds true, especially, for motivation. As indicated earlier, you can lead a horse to water, but you cannot make him drink unless you drink it yourself.

▸ Lastly, it is also very important for managers to work towards developing leadership qualities in people at all levels of the organization. Create more leaders who can take-on greater responsibility, and share your burden of work.

▸ The best leader is he who "leads like a baby". Even though a baby is totally helpless and dependent on the household, he is still the focus of all attention in the house - he is the king of the household - he leads the house.

M-3: GIVE THEM INFORMATION

▸ One of the primary causes of worker de-motivation is the unavailability of adequate information about the work environment. Workers formulate their attitudes about work and about the management on the basis of their cognitive evaluation of the available information. If the information is insufficient or lacking in authenticity, their feelings towards the work environment would normally be antagonistic in nature. This negativistic overture then becomes responsible for their lack of enthusiasm and drive for self-improvement.

► Every organization has many types of information and data, some of which are of a highly sensitive nature. It is not being suggested that all types of information be revealed to every worker. The idea here is to ensure that all relevant information requisite to the effective functioning of the processes for which the worker is responsible, should be readily available. For example, such information may include: any new machinery or processes being installed, changes to procedures, organizational changes that may impact the worker, any new programs or systems being considered for implementation, changes in job levels or renumerations, restructuring plans, etc.

► When proper information is available to the employees, they will make better cognitive evaluation of the situation, and their emotive reactions and attitude will be healthy and positive. In the absence of reliable information directly forthcoming from the management, the workers attempt to gather as much information as they can from any other reliable or unreliable source. Most often, workers end-up collecting inaccurate information from the corridor murmurs and rumours, and consequently they end-up formulating misleading cognitive evaluations, that result into forming negative mindset. Managers must intervene in this process and ensure that workers are provided up-to-date, timely, relevant, and accurate information. Employees wish to know what's happening around the work environment of which they are an integral part. They yearn for the feeling of belonging. When there is operational transparency in their functions and they sense that the management considers them as part of the family, they would, indeed, reciprocate by giving their personal best for the welfare of the family - the organization.

M-4: GIVE THEM SUPPORT

► For continuous motivation enhancement, better performance, and higher productivity, workers need ongoing management support - physical, emotional, and moral.

► Physical support encompasses: proper technology, adequate resources, requisite tools, suitable procedures, etc. A deficiency in any one of these causes a double jeopardy - the operational output is sub-optimal, and the workforce gets demotivated. Also included in this category are such support functions as : proper training and development, suitable working conditions, healthy work environment, physical amenities requisite to the safe and efficient operability.

▸ The role and importance of continuous training and retraining needs to be further accentuated - continuous training and development is by far the single most important entity for operational efficiency, innovativeness, and continuous enhancement of the workplace.

▸ For every work assignment, management must also endeavour to provide: clear set of directions, tailored guidelines, simple road maps, proper assignment of roles and responsibilities, adequate physical/financial/technical resources, and effective leadership.

▸ Another important entity required for generating a high motivational and high performance work environment, is supportive culture. By this we mean: everyone helping and supporting everyone else in any way possible and not working against each other, cross-functional participation and support, team work, cross-functional projects for improvement and innovation, etc.

▸ Finally, people need continued encouragement and moral support to undertake projects that would lead to improvement of processes and procedures. Even in routine work assignments, employees continuously look forward to encouragement and moral support from the management for a job well done.

M-5: GIVE THEM OWNERSHIP

▸ There is a sense of pride for every worker to say, "this is my job and I am going to do it well".

▸ Give the ownership of processes to the workers who are really and physically going to do the job anyway. Let the people run the systems and not systems driving people.

▸ Empower people. Establish team infrastructure at all levels of the hierarchy. Let teams solve problems, make decisions, and find innovative ways to carry on their operations in the most effective manner.

▸ Once the teams have identified some resource requirements to complete the task effectively, it is then the management's responsibility to ensure that adequate resources are made available to the workers. If this is not adequately done, the whole purpose of teamwork becomes redundant.

M-6: GIVE THEM OPPORTUNITY

▸ Most employees have a mission in life, and one of the predominant feature of that mission is growth and success. In an organization where there is very little opportunity for growth and development, the workers cannot realize and fulfil their expectations. In situations like this, workers have very little enthusiasm and drive for motivation, innovativeness or better performance. Since there is no room to grow, workers become robotic and uncreative in nature.

▶ Everyone needs to grow and improve - managers as well as workers. Just as much as the managers wish to excel and succeed, so do the workers. This realization should provide the management with an accentuated sense of responsibility to understand that: workers need adequate opportunities for growth and development, and they depend on the management's ability and initiative to generate an infrastructure for improvement.

▶ In addition to that, workers need challenge in their jobs. If the job is continuously routine in nature, the workers get bored and demotivated. The opportunity for growth, innovativeness, and creativity dissipates over time, resulting in low productivity and low morale. Management must evolve ingenious ways to create continuous challenge and enthusiasm in the job.

M-7: GIVE THEM CREDIT

▶ Every individual needs a pat on the back for job well done. That is an integral part of normal human behaviour. How often, as managers, have you praised and thanked your staff for their excellent contribution and performance? Motivation enhancement cannot be realized as long as we take the workers for granted and feel that to produce optimum results is a mandatory part of the workers' job and, therefore, there is no need to give them any extra credit for that.

▶ Trust, respect, and credit - when and where it is due, must be given. This should be the management's top priority. These are the most forceful and low-cost motivators of the workplace. Recognize the worker's performance as quickly as you recognize his mistakes.

▶ Recognition doesn't have to be a special, pre-planned effort or a special project - it is something that needs to be done routinely at the spur of the moment. Recognition doesn't even need any new equipment or procedures. It doesn't have to be complicated - a simple gesture can be enough. Praise should be sincere, specific, personal, positive, proactive, and it should be done as soon as it is requisite - it should not be postponed to a later date or suitable time.

▶ Contemplate on this fact in another way - you can provide only two types of entities to a worker: physical things or mental reinforcements. As managers, you know well the bare realities of the business life, that you cannot possibly keep providing physical entities to workers to maintain their motivation threshold, such as: bonuses, salary increase, promotions, incentives, rewards, opportunities for advancement, or other tangible perks. I mean, you can do these to some feasible extent, but you cannot continuously carry out these benevolent deeds forever. Also, it is not a good healthy practice to associate the inducement of motivation to the provision of tangible physical benefits - that is to say, that motivation would only happen if there are physical incentives and rewards, or else it won't happen. So instead, why don't you concentrate on the mental reinforcement aspects for inducing motivation - they are free - they won't even cost you anything. In this respect you have to think in terms of human behaviour - what elevates a person's ego - what makes him happy, enthusiastic, and satisfied - what drives him towards self-discipline and excellence, etc. Make a list of these entities, such as the following, and utilize your management prerogative and skills to exploit the usefulness and power of these mental stimulators to generate motivation:

- Empowerment through teamwork
- Environment of openness and trust
- Operational transparency
- Infrastructure for open communication
- Availability of proper information
- Assigning more responsibility
- Giving respect and credit
- Appreciation for a job well done

MANAGEMENT TQM SYPNOSIS

I would now summarize the gist of the above discussion so as to reinforce the message:

- ▸ Management bears profound responsibility for helping to generate worker motivation.
- ▸ Management must take the initiative and lead role in the process of motivation.
- ▸ Management must continuously and actively participate in the process of motivation.
- ▸ Workers have some fundamental needs which are intricately associated with their drive for motivation. Management must be fully cognizant of these needs and must endeavour to fulfil these needs:
  - Operational transparency
  - Availability of factual information
  - Management support

- Management commitment and trust
- Supportive culture
- Opportunities for growth
- Credibility and respect
▸ Management should encourage workers to achieve self-discipline, self-reliance, and a sense of responsibility.
▸ Management should establish an infrastructure for teamwork and empowerment.
▸ Management should provide effective leadership, as well as endeavour to generate leadership qualities in workers to accept greater responsibility.

To further strengthen these obligations, I would like to encapsulate the message via a beautiful simile. Consider a very small child - the child needs three things to grow into healthy adulthood: food, security, and love. Workers are like children when it comes to motivation - they need the same three entities as it pertains to their work environment, such as:

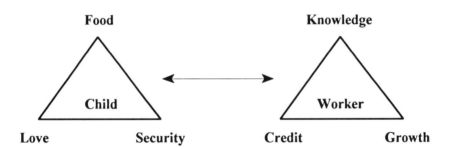

▸ Food: Knowledge, training, tools, support systems
▸ Love: Appreciation, trust, support, credit
▸ Security: Job security, stability, operational transparency, opportunities for growth

12

ACTION PLAN:
THE INFRASTRUCTURE

INTRODUCTION

Most of the earlier chapters have been devoted to a wide range of aspects pertaining to the softer side of management for improving motivation, job efficiency, and employee/employer relationship. What we now need to do is to establish an infrastructure to implement these intangible initiatives, as well as outline some tangible programs and systems for improving worker motivation. These two aspects are respectively elucidated in this and the next chapter.

Since not all forms of infrastructure or programs are necessarily applicable or conducive to every organization's operability framework and culture, we recommend that the organization must evaluate the viability and suitability of each undertaking before its acceptance and implementation. Some of the items to consider for evaluation include:

- ▸ What is the initiative? Is it compatible with our goals, mission, culture, and operability framework?
- ▸ How would it be administered? Do we have an implementation plan?
- ▸ Who will be responsible?
- ▸ How would it be effectively communicated to everyone?
- ▸ How would we measure its performance and effectiveness?

THE INFRASTRUCTURE

What do we need to accomplish our goal? As indicated repeatedly, there are only two parties involved in the human business management duel - the management and the workers. So obviously, what we need to do is to highlight the actions and initiatives that the management has to undertake, and identify the role an individual has to play Also, since many programs fail because of a lack of identifiable unit or entity with which the individual worker can establish a link for personal problem resolution, we are going to recommend the establishment of such a unit.

As a minimum, the following basic framework should be established:

- **Motivation Clinic:** A unit should be established in the organization that can provide an identifiable shelter/shrine for the workers, where they can comfortably go to get personal help. We would like this unit to be known to everyone in the organization as the "Motivation Clinic".
- **Team A Infrastructure - Management Team(s):** The function of this team is to evaluate the management's roles, responsibilities, and input into the process of human business management.
- **Team B Infrastructure - Worker Team(s):**
  - Team B-1 - Process Improvement Teams (PITs): These teams are worker-driven, worker-managed teams in all operational areas, to improve processes.
  - Team B-2: The function of these teams is to resolve personal-oriented problems of workers.
- **Team C Infrastructure - Cross-Functional Team(s):**
  - Team C-1: Joint management/worker teams to resolve issues pertaining to process improvement.
  - Team C-2: Joint management/worker teams to resolve issues relating to personal aspects of workers.
- **Team D Infrastructure - Senior Executive Team:** The function of this team is to discuss and resolve:
  - issues relating to the managers
  - issues identified by managers in their own Team A infrastructure
  - issues identified through the cross-functional Team C infrastructure
  - issues of general strategic importance
  - issues pertaining to all of the operational, functional, and organizational aspects of the organization.
- **Checklists - Management Introspective/Retrospective Checklist:** These checklists are to be used by managers to: identify the effectiveness of their own actions and efforts for motivating people, and to identify worker's state of motivation and level of satisfaction with the work environment.
- **Checklists - Worker Introspection Checklist:** This checklist is to be used by workers to identify, for themselves, their own efforts towards generating self-motivation and self-discipline.

This is just one possible schemata of teams and checklists that can be created to implement motivation enhancement initiatives. The list is by no means exhaustive. Organizations can add or realign this infrastructure as per their own requirements.

What we shall do now is to expand on these items one by one to provide more details on the functioning of these entities. No attempt is being made here to provide any ready-made guidelines or checklists - they must be generated by each organization itself, as per their own requirements. Every organization has different sets of needs, and the committee structure should be customized to reflect the organization's own human business management practices.

MOTIVATION CLINIC

This unit would be the most essential entity of the organization for human business management development. The clinic would have multi-dimensional functions, some of which include the following:

- For a start, a unit like this would serve as an internal marketing tool, for the organization, to identify its open-door policy and culture.
- The unit would be like a club - a think-tank place - a place to meet and discuss issues pertaining to the general welfare of the workers.
- It would serve as an identifiable place where workers can freely come to for any personal/occupational problems.
- The clinic can be responsible for handling many problems, such as: personal, work-stress related, or problems of psychophysiological or psychosomatic nature.
- The clinic can be responsible for arranging regular meetings, rap sessions, talks, seminars, or workshops, on such issues as stress management, motivation enhancement, work/life balance, burnout, change management, etc.
- The clinic can also undertake the task of carrying out opinion surveys to identify worker satisfaction and motivation levels. The results of these surveys would become an item of discussion in the meetings of various team infrastructures, as appropriate.
- The clinic can handle the grievance or suggestion program of the organization.
- The clinic can also manage social programs for employees or get-togethers for various occasions.

TEAM A INFRASTRUCTURE - MANAGEMENT TEAMS

These are one or several of the teams, as appropriate, comprising of the managers in all areas of work. They would meet once a month or as frequently as required, to discuss all relevant aspects relating to the human business management initiatives and programs. These committees are somewhat like the steering groups that provide guidance and input to the various Team B and C infrastructures. In as much as possible, the following items should at least become the core of their discussions:

- As management, are we all collectively committed to the motivation initiatives and programs? How do we demonstrate this commitment to the workers?
- Are we providing sufficient hands-on management participation into the program?
- Has the company's mission been adequately disseminated to everyone in the organization? How can we verify that everyone is working towards the common shared vision?
- Are workers familiar with the organization's goals and objectives?
- Are we providing effective leadership role to the workers? Can we tangibly identify exactly what we are doing in that direction?
- How do we verify that the worker is happy on the job?
- Do we make all necessary information available to workers?
- Have we looked into the working conditions for the employee to see what improvements can be made?
- Are working procedures well written and simple to apply?
- Are the technological aspects of work adequately suitable?
- Do workers have adequate resources to do their job effectively?
- Are the support systems adequate?
- Have we routinely assessed the training needs of employees?
- What opportunities for training and development are available to employees?
- Do we know the strengths and weaknesses of our employees?
- Who are the leaders in our workforce?
- Have we empowered people to control their own processes?
- Is there an effective team infrastructure in place?
- How innovative and self-motivated are our people?
- What kind of opportunities for growth have we provided?
- What are some of the tangible ways in which we can manifest our commitment and support for the welfare of our employees?
- How often have we involved the worker groups into our strategic planning framework to share our concerns and to help us in establishing our priorities?
- What kind of incentives have we identified for workers who demonstrate excellence?
- How often have we given credit where credit's due?

These are just some of the key aspects that should become the main focus of the management group for identifying what needs to be done for developing and implementing a successful motivation program.

TEAM B INFRASTRUCTURE: WORKER TEAMS

This structure has two sets of teams: Teams B-1 and Teams B-2. The Team B-1 infrastructure are the process improvement teams (PITs) that an organization would normally institute for production process improvement - except that, now their agenda will also include discussion of matters pertaining to motivation.

The Team B-2 infrastructure has to be carefully developed because of its sensitivity pertaining to personal-oriented problems of the workers. It can take any of the following format:

- ▸ One-to-one discussion with the supervisor or manager
- ▸ Discussion via the motivation clinic infrastructure
- ▸ Discussions via a team consisting of and operated by the workers themselves

TEAM C INFRASTRUCTURE: CROSS-FUNCTIONAL TEAMS

These are cross-functional teams comprising of selected members of Teams A and B infrastructures, and their function is to jointly address issues arising out of the deliberations of Team A and B infrastructures.

TEAM D INFRASTRUCTURE: SENIOR EXECUTIVE TEAM

As identified above, the function of this committee is to oversee the entire operational framework of the organization - managers, workers, technology, resources, etc. This committee is also responsible for the identification and development of potential managers from within the organization.

CHECKLISTS: MANAGEMENT

As a minimum, at least two types of checklists need to be developed.

- ▸ Management Input Checklist: Through this checklist, the managers would identify how effectively they are playing their role in inducing worker motivation and increasing worker loyalty and long-term commitment to the organization. We have appended above, under Team A Infrastructure, some probing questions that can be used to develop such a checklist.

- ▸ Worker Opinion Survey: This checklist is to be developed by management to gain an insight into a worker's level of satisfaction. It would include such items as:
  - • Worker's motivation level
  - • Worker's need hierarchy
  - • Worker's level of satisfaction with the overall work environment
  - • Worker's state of happiness
  - • Worker's level of work and life balance
  - • Worker's level of long-term commitment and loyalty towards the organization

CHECKLIST: WORKER

This checklist is a gauge for the workers to identify, through introspective analysis, how effectively they are playing their part for achieving self-motivation and self-discipline. There are two basic aspects that a worker has to contemplate upon:

- ▸ Matters that are personal and intrinsic to the individual
- ▸ Matters that are work-oriented and exert an impact on the operational aspects of work life

The introspective analysis for both categories would be, more or less, based on the questions and ideas appended in chapter 9.

Some of the entities pertaining to the worker's personal and intrinsic behaviour patterns that need to be examined include such items as:

- ▸ Personal attitude formation
- ▸ Attitude towards peers and management
- ▸ Enthusiasm and desire for participation in teamwork
- ▸ Accepting of challenge and responsibility
- ▸ Satisfaction with the nature and type of work
- ▸ Rapport with management
- ▸ Overall feeling of harmony with the work environment

Work-related aspects that a worker has to consider include the following:

- ▸ Work environment and working conditions
- ▸ Technical and technological aspects of work
- ▸ Work procedures
- ▸ Empowerment
- ▸ Adequacy and appropriateness of roles and responsibilities
- ▸ Training and development
- ▸ Opportunities for growth and development
- ▸ Availability of adequate information

- ► Effectiveness of inter and intra communication
- ► Management support
- ► Credit and incentives

A complete and thorough introspective analysis is imperative to the success of the program and for the realization of tangible improvements. The worker has to critically examine and evaluate all of these requisite entities in the most unbiased, mature, and judicious manner. Once the activity has been completed, the outcome could be segmented and handled in the following manner:

- ► Matters that are completely personal in nature would be worked out by the individual himself.
- ► Matters that are personal in nature but have a bearing on work life, would be discussed on a one-to-one basis with the immediate supervisor.
- ► Matters that are work-related would be passed on, through proper channels, to the appropriate teams for discussion and action.

To facilitate summarizing and documenting the results of the introspective analysis, a proforma like the one appended below, can be drawn-up. Suitable changes and modifications to this proforma can be made to customize it to your needs, or other appropriate proformas can be developed.

WORKER: INTROSPECTIVE PROFILE
☐ Items for Self-Improvement   ☐ Items for Discussion with Supervisors   ☐ Items for Discussion by Teams - A Infrastructure
Introspective Evaluation: Results
Action Taken
Improvements Made

IMPLEMENTATION SYNOPSIS

Let us now summarize the above discussion and identify the main steps of the overall implementation framework:

- ▸ Develop an overall profile of the program: need for the program; current deficiencies; perspective for motivation; expectations for the program; program parameters; program performance evaluation; program sustainability.
- ▸ Develop an infrastructure for worker introspection analysis: identification, evaluation, and improvement of matters relating to the workers personal and intrinsic aspects; identification and fulfilment of work-oriented needs.
- ▸ Develop an infrastructure for activities associated with the roles and responsibilities of the management towards the successful operation of the program.
- ▸ Develop a requisite infrastructure of teams and committees to operationalize the program mandate.
- ▸ Maintain requisite documentation and proformas.
- ▸ Ensure effective and requisite participation of all levels and all areas of the organization in the program.
- ▸ Encourage cross-functional interface, open and effective communication, and operational transparency.
- ▸ Empower the workforce to carry out the task of maintaining and improving the program.

13

ACTION PLAN:
THE INITIATIVES

THE RESOLVE

The previous chapter was devoted to establishing a suitable infrastructure to improve job efficiency. This chapter now outlines a variety of tangible and intangible initiatives and programs that an organization can undertake to enhance a worker's inner satisfaction, and ultimately his efficiency and loyalty to the organization.

Motivational initiatives create a sense of satisfaction in the individual that the organization cares. When a worker's goals are fulfilled, he feels indebted to the organization, and returns the favour through hard work, dedication, and long-term commitment. This creates a win/win situation for both parties - the organization caring for the individual, and the individual caring for the organization. And the more it happens, the more mutual satisfaction ensues.

It should also be borne in mind that there is also a lose/lose situation on the other end of the spectrum. This happens when, even after expending so much energy and resources to find a good person, an organization, somehow in mid-stream, forgets to look after an employee's needs and fails to recognize his contributions. The result - the employee quits, also in mid-stream - and both parties suffer - though the sufferings of the organization are far greater than that of the individual. The individual merely suffers from a temporary sense of instability. But, the organization looses a person who had a complete knowledge of the company's clients, technology, procedures, and overall business framework - someone hard to be replaced overnight. And worse, these employees may end up working for the company's clients or competitors. So evidently, the organization's loss is much bigger - they suffer in productivity and they have the hassle of finding another suitable person. So, the moral of the story is the same that we outlined in the beginning of the book:

"Organizations can have virtual guarantee of retaining their employees and achieving continued success, if ONLY they can keep motivating and challenging their employees with the SAME PASSION with which they hired them in the first place."

TANGIBLES VS. INTANGIBLES

There are two sets of actions that an organization can take to generate workforce motivation - tangibles and intangibles. Tangibles generally require financial resources in one form or another, while intangibles are almost cost-free. Examples of tangible actions include: promotions, advancement, financial rewards, bonuses, and other perks. The intangibles include: praise, recognition, empowerment, respect, responsibility, moral support.

Tangible entities are not only costly and resource depleting, they have a very short span of impact, and are untenable for achieving long-term motivation and commitment. Also, how far can an organization go in providing salary increases, promotions, and monetary rewards to employees on a continuous basis to induce motivation. And even if they can, it is not advisable to establish a precedence of expectations of a permanent one-to-one association between work and reward - that is, one happening only if the other happens.

Despite this fact, it is utterly surprising to note that a large majority of organizations are continuously busy developing and implementing high-powered tangible programs and systems for motivating their workforce, while totally ignoring to employ and utilize the intangible entities that are virtually cost-free. Even when we know that motivation is a human-dependent phenomenon, we still engage ourselves and feel proud and elated in establishing fancy-looking, costly, and highly mechanized and regimented systems for improving something that is totally a non-mechanized entity - the human attitude.

To get a perspective of our own idiosyncratic shortcomings, just contemplate on these thoughts: how often do we, as managers, go to an employee and say the following:

- ► How are you - is everything OK?
- ► Is there anything I can do to make your work more challenging and interesting?
- ► I would like to thank you for your help and contribution.
- ► Great job done - thank you very much.

- We are proud of you.
- We truly appreciate what you are doing.

The surprising fact is that all of these actions are absolutely free - they cost virtually nothing to the organization, and at the same time, they are the most powerful motivators for inducing permanent motivation mindset. Unfortunately, our contact with our workers is generally limited to those occasions when there is a problem and we need to intervene to take a punitive action.

On the list of intangibles, there are many cost-free things we can do, as for example:

- Create process improvement teams to let workers solve their own problems and accept greater responsibility.
- Allow greater control and decision-making authority to the workers for, at least, the processes that are directly under their supervision and for which they are solely responsible.
- Establish what we call "Motivation Clinics" to help workers achieve greater job satisfaction and better work-life balance.

The point we are making is that we must put greater emphasis on the intangible humanistic-oriented actions and initiatives, for they are the only means to bring about a permanent change in an individual attitude and performance mindset. There are three types of initiatives we shall be outlining in this chapter:

- Tangible actions which satisfy the worker's physical needs, leading to mental satisfaction.
- Intangible actions which bring mental satisfaction.
- Tangible initiatives that lure and bind a person for longer-term commitment to the organization.

A word of advice is in order here - that, the initiatives and programs outlined in this chapter are generic in content, and they need to be customized vis-a-vis the organization's needs and goals. Also, not all initiatives may be directly applicable or applicable without appropriate modifications, to all organizations at large. Each organization must carefully examine the initiative, evaluate its compatibility to their culture and operational framework, develop an appropriate strategic plan - and, if everything seems befitting - then implement the plan with total passion and commitment. Whatever you decide, you must execute the effort with enthusiasm and determination - for, efforts with half-hearted beginnings always end in failure.

ZERO TOLERANCE MANAGEMENT (ZTM):
THE 2-F PRINCIPLE

Before we begin to outline the various type of initiatives and incentives that the organization can consider, we would like to present a type of management style that we think may be the norm of the day in the new economic order - we are annotating it as: "Zero Tolerance Management (ZTM)". The underlying principle of ZTM are the two Fs: Freedom and Fear.

Freedom means that the organization is willing to give you almost virtual total freedom, within the possible confines of operational constraints, to do what you want to do. This would include many entities, some of which are:

- ▸ Empowerment, ownership, and control of processes
- ▸ Decision-making authority and responsibility for operations under your control
- ▸ Working on a flexible time schedule
- ▸ Managing of employee suggestion program
- ▸ Control over education and training
- ▸ Control over creative and innovative suggestions
- ▸ Control over acquisition of requisite technology
- ▸ Assistance with personal life situations
- ▸ Promotions, salary increases, bonuses, awards
- ▸ Recognition and appreciation
- ▸ Profit-sharing and better long-term financial assistance

However, there would be an element of "fear", as big and strong as "freedom" - that if you don't measure up to the expected norms and you make little contribution to the company's bottom line, then you are out of the company. It should be noted that this "fear" is not the same that people helplessly experience during other transitional changes that transpire within an organization, such as: downsizing, out-sourcing, mergers, or any other significant change that impacts the workforce. The fear that we are talking about here is the "responsibility-fear" - that is, if the person doesn't accept greater responsibility and accountability, even after having been giving absolute freedom, then there should be an element of fear of losing his/her job - not because of the organization - but because of his/her own shortcomings, deficiencies, or idiosyncrasies.

For the sake of brevity, we are only presenting just the basic fringes of the concept. The 2-F Principle needs to be formally elaborated with clear set of definitions of freedom and fear. Since the operational framework and culture of every organization is different, this concept has to be tailored for each company as per their needs and requirements.

PARTICIPATION ENHANCEMENT MINDSET

The first most important general task for the management is to think in terms of participatory management - to create a mindset and to find avenues to enhance worker/management participation. There are many ways to do that and we shall suggest a few as follows:

- ▶ Creating an infrastructure of teams to manage most of the operational aspects of business.
- ▶ Sharing information with workers on the health of the organization.
- ▶ Creating an infrastructure through which the worker's opinions and suggestions are solicited.
- ▶ Involving employees in the decision-making process for all operational and functional entities that impact the workers.
- ▶ The establishment of advisory committees involving employees at all levels of the organization.

Allowing greater participation by workers enhances the worker's morale and a sense of feeling that they are an integral and wanted part of the organization - the family. It imparts a sense of trust and responsibility - the two most essential elements for generating worker motivation and loyalty.

EMPOWERMENT

The next closely linked initiative pertains to ownership and empowerment. Once again, for this the organization has to develop an empowerment culture mindset. When a society becomes highly democratized and there is a prevailing sense of realization and trust in human strength and commitment, the only way to tap this enormous wealth of energy is through empowerment. Born out of a fairly natural and realistic progression of events, the concept of empowerment is still, perhaps, the most widely misunderstood entity of our times. Since people are the backbone of any organization, empowerment simply means trusting people and giving them the pride and the pleasure to utilize their potential to the fullest extent to create excellence. The following description should assist in dispelling any mystery or myth as to what empowerment means or does not mean.

Empowerment does not mean:

- That anyone can function/operate independently in isolation as he/she pleases
- Chaos/anarchy/end of monarchy/ abdication of throne/ coup d'etat
- That the manager is stripped of all his powers, authority and responsibility
- That there is no hierarchical infrastructure operating in the organization

Empowerment means

- Sharing a common vision
- Achieving collective benefit from individual expertise
- Creating excellence through teamwork
- Creating an integral cross-functional interface for goal accomplishment
- Enabling people to work freely and innovatively
- Letting people have the pride in workmanship
- Allowing people to accept process ownership and responsibility
- Enabling people to focus on strategic priorities
- Focusing on standardized and disciplined approach to solving problems
- Allowing people to focus on long-term strategic responsibilities while executing short-term actions

The spectrum of empowerment is very wide - it can range from a nominal involvement to a total self-directed working environment. Empowerment is a disciplined way of working in a partnering relationship - a give and take relationship. The management puts their trust in the workers' abilities, allows them to function freely and hopes to achieve excellence in all aspects of business operability. The worker, having been given the freedom, pride and privilege to function under an umbrella of shared responsibility, without hierarchical hang-ups, feels elevated and in turn attempts to provide his personal best for the welfare and success of the organization. In all simplicity, empowerment is a win/win approach to doing business. Summarizing, empowerment typically means:

- Responsibility
- Authority
- Process ownership
- Information
- Resources
- Accountability

JOB ENRICHMENT

One of the major reason for high job mobility is job dissatisfaction. Job dissatisfaction emanates from any or all of the following:

- ▸ Nature of work itself
- ▸ Working conditions and environment
- ▸ Management-related problems

When a person doesn't like his job, he feels trapped and suffocated. The work becomes demeaning and dehumanizing - and the worker becomes a mechanical unit, totally controlled and dispensable. He has two choices - to leave and go for another job that is more meaningful, or to remain in the present job and bear the quiet suffering. In the later case, the employee would become demotivated; won't perform to capacity; become frustrated and depressed; be more absent from work; and may ultimately become sick.

The following options can be exercised in this scenario:

- ▸ The management can fire the employee
- ▸ The employee can quit and look for another more meaningful job
- ▸ The management can take initiative to augment and enrich the job

The first two options are a poor solution to the problem - running away from responsible human management is not only an act of self-centred cowardliness, but it is also an exhibition of lack of self-confidence. If the organization fires a person, what would they do next? Hire another person - but what if the same problem persists? Hiring and firing cannot rectify the situation because the problem may not be with the person, but with the job itself. On the other side, if the employee quits the job, it is a clear manifestation of the worker's lack of open and honest communication with the management and a lack of empathy and loyalty.

The most optimal remedy involves the following:

- ▸ Open and honest communication between the worker and the management
- ▸ Mutual understanding, appreciation, and resolution of the problem
- ▸ Augmentation of the job through job re-engineering, job reallocation, job-rescheduling, etc.

In order to enrich the job, the organization has to know what makes the job monotonous and dislikable. Generally, workers dislike jobs that have very little challenge; are over-controlled; repetitive in nature and, therefore, requiring very little ingenuity. The humanization of work requires many actions and initiatives of varying degree, such as:

- Well-defined purpose and goals
- Adequate resources and support systems
- Management and cross-functional peer support
- Better controls
- Freedom to do things conducive to job excellence
- Recognition and appreciation
- Free flow of information, internal and external
- Job skill enhancement
- Job variety and creativity enhancement

To enrich and augment a job, three possible initiatives can be activated:

- To restructure the job in order to make it more challenging and motivating
- To reallocate the worker to another job that is more compatible with his skills
- To rearrange job logistics and worker schedule, so that there is more parity between the two

Let us now consider these initiatives one by one and expound on their viability and usefulness.

JOB RE -ENGINEERING

To effectively re-engineer a job, it is important to first identify the overall job variables, and their current strengths and weaknesses. Job restructuring may involve some or all of the following:

- Redesigning of the facility
- Redesigning of the layout
- Change in technology
- Acquisition of new technology
- Change in procedures
- Simplification of operations
- Elimination of repetitiveness
- Improving job variety and depth
- Change in responsibility structure
- Making the job more challenging and creative
- Optimal usage of worker's skills
- Shifting of controls and responsibility to workers

JOB REALLOCATION

This may involve either job sharing or job rotation. The management should identify the skills, knowledge, and experience of the worker and see where and in which job can the worker be optimally reallocated.

We have identified, in the preceding chapters, some guidelines on how management can understand personality characteristics of a person and utilize this information to place the person in a job for which he is most suitable.

For example, we indicated that there are three personality characteristics that bear the most profound impact on a person's operability framework: aggressiveness, maturity, and knowledge.

Then, there are three basic abilities that a person possesses - the abilities of brain, mouth, and hands. That is to say:

- ► Some people are good with their brains - scientists, research-oriented people, analysts, strategic planners, etc.
- ► Some people are good at speaking - coordinators, resource people, service and sales group, etc.
- ► Some people are handy - they are excellent craftsmen.

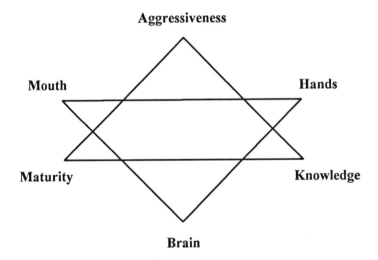

So, the ingenuity and ability of the management lies in deciphering the strength of a person's personality - and collating it with the person's ability to optimally allocate the person to the right job within the organization.

In addition, if a person needs further training to achieve suitability for job rotation or job reallocation, then the management should make sure that such training is made available to the individual.

BRAIN DOMINANCE AND JOB REALLOCATION

Similar to the above approach of combining personality factors and ability traits to develop an optimal profile of the individual, there is another initiative that is worth considering to improve job efficiency. Mr. Ned Hermann of the Hermann Institute in North Carolina has propounded a new theory which asserts that our brains have different areas and each area has different thinking patterns. He compartmentalizes the brain into four quadrants - A, B, C, and D - with quadrants A and B being on the left side of the brain, and quadrants C and D on the right. Since each quadrant performs a different function, depending on how we utilize each part of our brains, we may be operating on different wavelengths, with our own preferred thinking styles. Let us first examine how Hermann qualifies each compartment:

- ▸ **Quadrant A:** Responsible for logical and rational thinking. Persons in this category are: mathematicians, statisticians, analytical and informatics technicians - people who like to deal with facts and figures.
- ▸ **Quadrant B:** Responsible for organizational skills. This category includes people who like to plan, organize, control everything properly and sequentially - military personnel, strategic planners, etc.
- ▸ **Quadrant C:** Responsible for behavioural type of thinking. These are people-oriented people, who care for feelings, emotions, and basic human needs. They are aesthetic and spiritual in nature.
- ▸ **Quadrant D:** Responsible for creativity and innovation. Artists, musicians, etc., belong to this category.

Hermann contends that one of the reasons for job inefficiency and low productivity is sub-optimal placement of people - that is, people's thinking style not matching with the nature and type of work they are in. He has developed a set of questionnaires, known as Hermann Brain Dominance Instrument, through which one can evaluate a person's preferred pattern of thinking. The questionnaire helps to lay out a profile of a person's dominance patterns. With this knowledge, it is possible to accomplish the following:

- ▸ Reallocate the person to the job that is commensurate with his brain dominance pattern.
- ▸ Retrain the person to utilize several areas of the brain with equal dominance and evolve multi-dimensional capabilities in the person.

▸ Identify individuals who have the capability of utilizing all four quadrants of the brain, and earmark them for higher management positions.

For the sake of brevity, we are only making a brief mention of this method here. For any serious considerations of application of this technique, the reader should explore further details of the method.

JOB LOGISTICS

In addition to the above initiative, the organization can also examine if there are any logistics issues that affect the worker's job performance, motivation, or job satisfaction. The two entities that we are considering here are: flexitime and compressed hours. Both of these items need careful scrutiny before their application, because they may not be suitable for all organization en masse.

Flexitime means that a worker can choose his timings of coming and going to work to suit his personal life contingencies, as long as he is present in the office for the core time period when everyone must be at work. This entity has many advantages as well as disadvantages - therefore, organizations must carefully weigh the pros and cons of its applicability to their situation before adopting this program.

Advantages include:

▸ Workers can save commuting time by avoiding rush-hour traffic
▸ Personal life management can be easier
▸ Flexitime may help reduce stress due to urgency and lack of time
▸ Flexitime affords freedom and a relaxed mindset - and consequently, it improves the individual's attitude, behaviour patterns, and productivity.

Disadvantages include:

▸ Creates scheduling problems for meetings
▸ Requires additional resources to keep track of hours worked
▸ Creates problems of monitoring and supervision
▸ Employees may tend to abuse the freedom

The other initiative pertains to **compressed work hours**. This means that a worker can choose to alter his working schedule to gain more time for personal contingencies. Compressed work hours can take on any mutually agreeable time schedule, but the following two options are the ones most often exercised:

▸ A worker can work for 4 days, at 10 hours a day in a week, and take a Monday or Friday off.

▸ A worker can work 80 hours over a 9-day period, and take a Monday or Friday off every two weeks.

This sort of arrangement is quite beneficial to many workers, but it should be adopted only if it is mutually conducive to both the organization and the individual.

PROFIT SHARING PLANS

Many of the initiatives and incentives, including money, work very well for generating worker satisfaction over the short interval spans - but, for long-term commitment and loyalty, the organization has to consider initiatives that, in a way, lure and ethically bind an individual for a long-term retention. Programs of this nature are gaining momentum and popularity, and in many cases, are proving to be quite effective. All such programs have the following elements in common:

▸ Considering employees as equal partners and letting them share in the success of the company.
▸ Creating better renumeration policies and compensation programs to encourage worker loyalty.
▸ Making greater use of retention bonuses that recognize employee's skills, abilities, and knowledge.
▸ Generating a bonus pool that keeps the employees informed about company's profits and pays them a portion of profit-sharing at regular intervals.
▸ Making loan payments to the employees to help them make major purchases, for example, loans for down payment for buying a home - this would make them less likely to move to another area and hence would encourage long-term commitment.
▸ Creating some type of personally tailored retirement plans which offers self-directed benefits and better financial planning schemes.
▸ Creating some type of company-developed deferred profit-sharing plans tailored to meet the employee's needs.

There can be other similar initiatives and programs that an organization can create in line with their company's financial position and operational viability. The main function of all such programs can be stated as follows:

▸ It allows employees to have direct control over their financial affairs, as well as they can get free professional advice and guidance.
▸ These gestures by the company gives employees a feeling of confidence that the company cares - it also brings a sense of financial stability and control in their personal affairs.

Two plans that are becoming increasingly popular and gaining employee's acceptance are: Group Retirement Savings Plan (GRSP), and Deferred Profit Sharing Plan (DPSP).

GROUP RETIREMENT SAVINGS PLAN (GRSP)

Much like the individual retirement savings plan, the GRSP lets the employee decide the amount of contribution he would like to make, and these are done through automatic payroll deduction systems. The amount of deduction can be altered or stopped as per the employee's wishes. Also, the plan provides a wide variety of investment choices and once again, the employee decides on how these funds are to be invested. The benefits to the employee include:

- ▸ Reduction in income tax payments
- ▸ Saving for retirement
- ▸ Control over financial affairs
- ▸ Control over investment options

The benefits to the organization includes:

- ▸ Low administration and financial costs
- ▸ Very little company involvement and responsibility
- ▸ Excellent way to cement employee/employer relationship for long-term commitment

DEFERRED PROFIT SHARING PLAN (DPSP)

Another initiative worth looking into in conjunction with the GRSP is the DPSP, which is a cross between the pension plan and a retirement savings plan. In the DPSP, the employee does not make any contributions and the employer's contributions are in proportion to their profits. So, while the GRSP allows an employee to accumulate retirement savings, DPSP encourages employees to improve productivity and have the opportunity to get recognition of their abilities through profit-sharing.

Both of these plans, the GRSP and the DPSP, are profit-sharing plans which create a sense of financial stability for the employee - something that is very important for the employee's physical and mental needs and satisfaction. However, both plans are linked to how long an employee stays with the company. For example, an employee shall forfeit his rights to DPSP if he decides to leave the company. Thus, the plans create a win/win situation for both parties. The employer retains his employees and is spared of the agony and costs associated with continuous hiring. And the employee gains those benefits by exhibiting his loyalty to the organization.

For the sake of brevity, we are making a passing mention of these plans here - an organization wishing to consider implementation of these plans should investigate the matter further to formulate a plan of action that is most conducive to their operability framework.

MISCELLANEOUS LIST OF INITIATIVES

Finally, we are presenting a brief general description of some of the essential initiatives and programs that the organization can implement to enhance motivation.

RECOGNITION, PRAISE, REWARD

Monetary rewards are essential, but they only generate time-limited happiness and satisfaction. Next to money, recognition and praise are the most profound entities that today's workforce is looking for. Not only is it totally cost-free, continuous recognition is the motivator that generates long-term dedication.

It is my personal belief that the most important entities for us humans are the 2-Ms: Money and Meaning. Money need is short-lived - it comes and goes - but, the need for "meaning" is perpetual. We are always looking for greater meaning in our lives, whether it be in personal or occupational life. And, recognition is one entity that provides us the meaning for what we do. Because, praise and recognition touches our sensitivities, our consciousness, our psyche - and that's where our sense of fulfilment resides. Let us make our case more convincing by examining, a little further, the nature of recognition:

- ► You don't need anyone's permission to do it
- ► You don't need any new technology, equipment, or procedures
- ► You don't need any money or budget approvals
- ► It doesn't have to be complicated - even a simple gesture is enough

Surprisingly yet, how many managers seriously do it. They are all too busy in their own worries or in their endeavours to develop high powered systems that require new technology and budget approvals - to do what? - to reach the human psyche - something that can be done by a simple "thank you" note. The irony is that the more mechanical we are becoming, the more we are moving towards replacing personal touch by computer touch. And the more that is happening, the more employees are craving for human touch. So, in fact, the harder we are running to catch something, the further it is going from us.

Following is a list of some basic recommendations:

- ▸ The first most important thing is to create a recognition culture in the organization. Managers must increase their awareness about what workers think, how they behave, and what motivates them.
- ▸ Each manager starts the recognition process within his/her immediate sphere of influence.
- ▸ Recognition process should go step-by-step, person by person, and it must be focused, or else it will never be remembered.
- ▸ Praise is an entity which should be sincere, personal, specific, positive, timely, and proactive.
- ▸ Recognition is not a special project of limited shelf-life - it is something to be done continuously. And there is no need to look for perfection in this process.
- ▸ Involve people in the process - doing things with them is more important than doing for them. Make it a one-to-one exercise - ask them what motivates them, where would they want to go from here, and how can you, as managers, help them accomplish their goals.
- ▸ Make use of simple thing like:
  - • writing thank you notes
  - • wandering around in the work areas, talking to people, observing, recognizing, praising, and encouraging
  - • schedule specific time slots for recognition
  - • delegate and assign specific responsibility to your staff for recognition
  - • keep an open-door, accessible, approachable working milieu
- ▸ At the team level, recognition can include things like:
  - • participation in the team work
  - • recognizing and announcing team success with fanfare
  - • praising everyone
  - • praising the team leader
  - • establishing recognition awards
  - • celebrating success
- ▸ Establish a graduated recognition/applause program, with graduations such as: satisfactory achievement, extraordinary achievement, distinguished achievement, etc. And then, each level of achievement can be associated with some kind of recognition, award, or monetary benefit.

- Use the concept of "visual factory" for recognition. This means visual display of recognition, throughout the organization, of a worker's achievements, through such means as:
  - putting names of achievers on company billboards
  - publishing the achiever's ideas, achievements, and their name and picture in the internal bulletin or magazine
  - calling a special meeting or having a special party to honour the achiever
- Employee recognition can take many shapes and forms, such as:
  - public praise
  - morale-building meetings
  - promotion for performance
  - distributing pens, t-shirts, pads/papers, with the achiever's name
  - sending flowers to the achiever's house to let the immediate family know how much the organization cares
  - creating a "club of achievers", which employees can join only through high achievement - this will set up an internal desire among people to work hard, prove their dedication, and earn the club membership.

OPINION SURVEYS

As a minimum, at least two types of surveys must be continuously conducted by the management:

- **Internal Surveys:** To determine the level of motivation and satisfaction of employees with regard to management attitude and support, work environment, work itself, and other related matters. This survey should also be able to identify what motivates workers and what would workers like changed or augmented in the organization to achieve better results for themselves as well as for the organization.
- **External Surveys:** These surveys are carried out by management to keep themselves abreast with the working conditions, salaries, benefits, and other related entities offered by the employers in similar market segments. With the knowledge gained from such surveys, the organization can realign and improve their own infrastructure to look after their employees justly and equitably so as to earn their long-term retention and loyalty.

EMPLOYEE ASSISTANCE PROGRAM (EAP)

A good employee assistance program can take on several employee-related issues in which management can help and contribute toward's employee's welfare. Some of these include:

- ▸ Financial assistance to employees for specific purposes
- ▸ Personal counselling
- ▸ Counselling on work-related issues
- ▸ Counselling on stress-related issues
- ▸ Childcare and daycare issues
- ▸ Leave policy concerning family-related matters

All of these types of efforts leave a strong permanent positive impact on the worker's attitude and satisfaction level, and this helps to make the employee/employer relationship stronger and enduring.

TOTAL WELLNESS PROGRAM (TWP)

Workforce stress is not just a fictional entity, it is a virtual reality of every workplace. It presents the greatest danger to the worker's health and a threat to higher productivity. Stress brings about a slow, painful, and unnoticed death of the worker's enthusiasm and energy. It builds up over time, leading to depression and possible illness in a person.

What causes stress at the workplace? Many factors, small and big, cause workforce blues, but it is really the collective impact of several factors that bring about the final demise. Such factors include: bad managers, too many changes in too short a time, bad working conditions, the nature of the work itself, etc.

Organizations can play a very important role in this regard. In fact, organizations should make relentless efforts to alleviate or minimize workforce stress, because it is really to their own advantage to do so. Rather than trying to improve productivity as a stand-alone entity, they should try to improve a person's mental and physical health, and the productivity improvement will come by automatically. Many organizations are cognizant of this reality, and they have instituted good total wellness programs. Some of the things that can be done in this regard include such entities as:

- ▸ In-house counselling facilities - these can be accommodated through the "motivation clinic", as described earlier.
- ▸ In-house wellness and health improvement programs.
- ▸ One-to-one interventions by the managers.
- ▸ Memberships to external health clubs and associations.

EMPLOYEE SUGGESTION PROGRAM (ESP)

The ESP is a very important undertaking an organization can consider to improve productivity. The program brings benefits to all parties: the organization, the employees, the customers, and the stakeholders. The fundamental benefits of an ESP are as follows:

▸ Improved quality
▸ Increased creativity
▸ Greater participation
▸ Improved morale
▸ Greater job satisfaction
▸ Improved revenues

For optimum results, the program must be formally structured, introduced, and operated. Some essential steps in the development of such a program include the following:

▸ Develop the basic infrastructure: concurrence of management and workers; creating a unit with designated responsibility; creating a steering council to make decisions on the selection of ideas, etc.
▸ Develop the goals and operational framework of ESP.
▸ Explain the program to the employees and train them on how the program works.
▸ Involve everyone in the program.
▸ Establish infrastructure for maintaining the program, and measuring its efficiency.
▸ Establish a reward/recognition system for good suggestions.
▸ Monitor the benefits accrued from the suggestions.
▸ Publicize results for accentuating and promoting the program.

TOGETHERNESS PROGRAM (TP)

Getting together with people is not only fun, but it has some very significant benefits for both the organization and its employees. The following few points may be noted:

▸ It breaks the ice that stands between the management and the workers, and blocks free flow of communication.
▸ It imparts a sense of warmth and being wanted, to the employees.
▸ It clearly identifies the existence of a democratized workplace, and the company's participative and supportive culture.
▸ People feel part of the family.
▸ The TP sets in motion the happiness of a worker, his motivation, his dedication and commitment to the organization.

The togetherness program can take many forms, such as:

- ► Getting together of groups of workers with their supervisors or managers, within each unit, over a cup of coffee or over the lunch hour.
- ► Getting together to play games together.
- ► Getting together for other activities, for example, during presentation of recognition awards, etc.
- ► General social get-togethers for the entire organization.

14

THE EPILOGUE

THE FINALE

And now the finale! Let us complete the loop - we started with the prologue - with a number of challenging questions about our modus operandi in tackling the issues of worker motivation and retention - and after a lengthy discussion, I hope that we have a better realization of the dilemma and a clearer understanding of the task at hand. In this final epilogue, we shall summarize our subject-matter discussion by recapitulating the realism, the reason, and the resolve.

THE SYPNOSIS

- ▶ We began with the most basic reality of the business world - the desire to achieve success - which translates itself into profitability and continued growth.
- ▶ To achieve this goal, the organization must have, as a minimum:
  - state-of-the-art technology
  - adequate infrastructure
  - efficient systems and procedures
  - a skilled and motivated workforce
- ▶ Most important determinant of success:
  - highly productive, committed, and motivated workforce
- ▶ Major problems of human business management:
  - how to find good people
  - how to motivate them
  - how to keep them for long-term commitment
- ▶ The process of retention:
  - retention is a by-product of motivation

- ○ motivation is a by-product of happiness
- ○ happiness is a by-product of goal-fulfilment
- ► Solution to the problem lies in:
  - • identifying goals of the individual and the organization
  - • striving for goal compatibility
  - • satisfying the individual's goals
  - • finding avenues to challenge and motivate the worker
- ► Goals of the organization:
  - • making money: higher productivity
  - ○ making more money: expanding market share
  - • making more money continuously: greater market credibility
- ► Goals of the individual:
  - • money
  - • work environment
  - • work itself
  - • self esteem
  - • security
  - ○ work-life balance
  - • advancement
  - ○ fulfilment
- ► Individual's responsibility:
  - • develop the self
  - • accept greater responsibility
  - • generate self-motivation, self-discipline
  - • inculcate a positive attitude, performance mindset, and passion for excellence
- ► Organization's responsibility:
  - • accept greater participatory sense of responsibility towards the workforce
  - • generate better management skills and capabilities
  - • develop intangible initiatives to fulfil the employee's aspirations
  - • develop tangible initiatives to motivate and gain an employee's trust and long-term loyalty and commitment
- ► The approach: some lessons for the management
  - • Give and thou shalt receive. The more you give, the more you shall receive.
  - • Giving doesn't have to be in dollar-value only; it can be in kind. A bit of both is required for balance, as appropriate.
  - • Accentuate on the intangibles (cost-free) efforts to motivate, challenge, and fulfil the employee.

- Develop tangible (cost-associated) initiatives to gain an employee's long-term commitment to the organization.
- Develop proper infrastructure, operational as well as organizational, to put in place the intangibles and the tangibles.
- Humanize the workplace - maintain the human touch - the sense of belonging - the family feeling.
- Keep systems simple.
- Let the systems be people-developed, people-driven, people-managed.
- Don't emphasize on systems; emphasize on people for whom the systems are created.

ESSENTIALS OF PERSONAL/ORGANIZATIONAL SUCCESS

PERSONAL GROWTH	PERSONAL SUCCESS
The 10 Absolutes	**The 10 Commandments**
1. Trust God	1. Have a personal vision
2. Trust others	2. Keep positive attitude
3. Trust Yourself	3. Have self confidence
4. Love life	4. Have courage to face any challenge
5. Be happy	5. Develop multi-skill capability
6. Be helpful	6. Accept responsibility
7. Think big	7. Develop organizational ability
8. Be humble	8. Commit to the cause
9. Be compassionate	9. Have determination to achieve the task
10. Be forgiving	10. Develop passion for excellence

SELF CONFIDENCE	
The 10 Rules	
1. Know yourself	6. Stop living comparatively
2. Accept Yourself	7. Compete with yourself
3. Learn continuously	8. Have courage to speak your mind
4. Accept criticism positively	9. Develop an attitude of confidence
5. Avoid destructive self-criticism	10. Feel good about yourself

---

SELF-DISCIPLINE

The 10 Axioms

1. Prepare an action plan everyday
2. Develop "to do" checklist
3. Separate out the "musts" and the "wishes"
4. Objectify expectations
5. Proceed from the manageables to the unmanageables
6. Take decisive decisions and actions
7. Stop procrastinating
8. Have the determination to complete tasks
9. Accept nothing less than the best
10. Measure performance each day

SUCCESSFUL MANAGER

The 10 Essentials

1. Ability to organize
2. Ability to lead and delegate
3. Ability to take decisions
4. Courage to take risk and responsibility
5. High positive energy and drive
6. Ability to perform under pressure
7. Multi-dimensional skills capability
8. High performance mindset and passion for excellence
9. Compassion and judiciousness
10. Balanced and stable personality

WORKFORCE MOTIVATION

Top 10 Tangible (Cost-Associated) Motivators

1. Opportunity for growth and advancement
2. Rewards
3. Profit-sharing plans
4. Health and fitness programs
5. Work-life balance opportunities
6. Assistance programs
7. Family benefit programs
8. Health plans
9. Retirement plans
10. Togetherness programs

WORKFORCE MOTIVATION
Top 10 Intangible (Cost-Free) Motivators   1. Interesting, challenging, and meaningful work   2. Controls and decision-making responsibility   3. Management trust and support   4. Respect, recognition, and praise   5. Fear free freedom   6. Personal touch and attention   7. Operational transparency   8. Participatory environment   9. Supportive culture   10. Organizational culture, values and beliefs

THE LAST WORD

The basic common core of business success is that single most important entity - the human endeavour. Human endeavour comes from human motivation. But motivation is an attitude-dependent phenomenon that is generated from within the individual, by the individual. Although, motivation seems to be more intrinsic rather than extrinsic, yet its generation is only possible and plausible when both intrinsic and extrinsic forces - management and individual workers - join hands together to work in harmony.

Management must understand that just talking about motivation or brooding over it actionlessly won't bring any results. Motivation cannot just spring-up by itself - you have to work hard for it - which means, making some concerted efforts, implementing some powerful initiatives, and making a serious commitment to purpose. A well-developed plan of action, a suitable program, worker participation, and managements's unsolicited input - these are some of the important ingredients for workforce motivation enhancement.

The intrinsic forces - the worker's own internal dedication and commitment is even more important for the motivation process. Workers have to generate a self-directed impetus to be wanting to achieve motivation, excellence, and success. And the interesting part of the story is that, while management has to undertake some tangible tasks, such as developing a more aggressive role and sense of responsibility and creating some initiatives, the worker has virtually nothing more to do than merely exercising his own will to do things. Doing that doesn't even cost anything to the worker - it's free for the asking.

How is it free for the worker - I want to expand on this and close my discussion be presenting two intriguingly funny, but scientifically true, metaphors. Firstly, workers don't need any extra brain power to exercise Personal TQM - because, scientists tell us that we are only using about 15% of our given brain capacity - we, therefore, don't need any more brain, we just have to utilize more of what we already have. And, the simplest way to do that is to expand our horizon and our satisfaction level. Already, our brain capacity exceeds our expectations - make it the other way around - let loose your expectations to exceed your brain capacity - let your expectations surpass your experience.

Secondly, and even more amusing, scientists are now beginning to tell us that we have two brains, and not just one. The first brain is our regular familiar brain that is encased in our skull. But, they say that there may be another lesser known, but vitally important, brain that sits in our gut. The gut's brain, known as the "enteric nervous system", is located in sheaths of tissue lining the esophagus, stomach, small intestines and colon. Considered as a single entity, it is packed with neurons, neurotransmitters and proteins that zap messages between neurons, support cells like those found in the brain proper and a complex circuitry that enables it to act independently, learn, remember and, as the saying goes, produce gut feelings.

I am not too concerned about the physiological aspects of these theories - I am more interested in using these analogies for my Personal TQM and motivation paradigm - to plead that personal excellence is all about psycho-physiological awakening of the "gut brain" and greater utilization of the regular "skull brain". **Amen!**

THE IMPERATIVES OF BUSINESS SUCCESS

THE SECOND RENAISSANCE

In business, everything is connected to everything else. You cannot implement and operate systems disjointedly and hope to achieve global business success. You have to consider all systems integratively and then develop your strategies to maximum your output and profitability. So, in addition to studying the subject of human business management, what we also wish to do in this chapter is to look at the business operability from a total, whole perspective, and recommend some new paradigms of business success for the new millennium.

For every organization, small or large, public or private, business success is a conscious decision to exceed the limits. Such a decision, indeed, calls for a high degree of continual dedication and regimentation to the basic principles of sensible management. To develop an effective business plan, we need to do the following:

- ► Evaluate the viability of our current initiatives
- ► Examine the suitability of our current strategies vis-a-vis the demands and pressures of the impending environment
- ► Identify the strengths and weaknesses of our systems
- ► Develop a suitable strategic framework

The failure of our systems, as indicated earlier, is really due to either the inability of our systems to operate integratively and/or to their inadequacy to accommodate and be effectively aligned with the changes that transpire in the business environment. The most effective strategic plan for business operability is always the one that is built on the experiences of the past. These experiences are then meshed with the impending realities and predicaments to evolve a winning futuristic strategic framework. Let us do precisely that - recapitulate what we did in the past, identify future shocks, and see what we have to do differently or better than before to achieve "competitive success".

STATE OF THE GLOBAL UNION

Speaking of the changing face of the marketplace - the second millennium is coming to an end. We have, indeed, witnessed quite a few significant events: Greek and Roman civilizations, the Renaissance, world wars, the Industrial Revolution, the Quality Revolution - to name just a few. In fact, the last 50 to 100 years have been scaringly dramatic in terms of changes. The amount of changes witnessed in this century alone far exceeds the cumulative changes which occurred over the past several centuries. Probably the most significant change we are facing today is change itself - we seem to be in a state of perpetual movement. Most of these changes have been very unpredictable, fast, and revolutionary in nature. These non-human changes virtually took us by surprise. We were running amuck trying to manage in a rush, without the benefit of any historical precedence and assistance. We were frantically developing and inventing models and systems as well as resorting to all kinds of frenzied actions like: restructuring, re-engineering, downsizing, etc. - all with good intentions, of course. Hopefully, we are a bit more matured now - more stable and opulent. We know that one-size model/system-fits-all is not going to work - we have to think in terms of diversity, customization, integration, flexibility, and adaptability.

FUTURE SHOCK

Predicting the future is as difficult as standardizing morality. However, with whatever sign-posts we can see, it is possible to identify with a fairly good degree of confidence, the expected constraints and predicaments of the impending environment - the second renaissance. Let us enumerate a few paradigm shifts:

- ▸ Global competitiveness that was ushered in about two decades ago, will continue unabated.
- ▸ We are witnessing a new revolution - the telecommunication and computer revolution - we are heading into the information age and network society.
- ▸ The new workforce is: highly democratized, knowledge-based, independent, self-sufficient, and empowered.

So the question is: what do we do - where do we go from here? That is precisely what we want to address here. We are going to outline a grand integration plan for the overall business operability, which we think is imperative for business success in the next century.

THE TEN SUCCESS IMPERATIVES

With this as the basis of our understanding, we have collated, after a considerable thought, observation, and experiential evaluation, a set of postulates that we believe are fundamental to the success of any organization in the impending new millennium. The basic framework of the guiding principles outlined here have been derived from the knowledge and experience we have gained from the system management deficiencies and idiosyncrasies of our past actions. For that reason, these imperatives portray our futuristic action implicitly eulogized through the eyes of our past actions. We shall now expound on these imperatives through a birds-eye view of what we encountered during the course of our experience, and also identify what mid-course corrections we must undertake to move towards the right direction

BUSINESS SUCCESS IMPERATIVES	
The 10 Imperatives	**Principle of "Sensible Management"**
1. Commitment to Purpose	1. Shared Management
2. Future Scanning	2. Integrative Operability
3. Dynamic Customer Orientation	3. Self-Directed Systems
4. Operational Competencies	4. Operational Simplicity
5. Quality Excellence	5. Continuous Training
6. Personal Excellence	6. Process Improvement Focus
7. Continual Improvement Mindset	7. Performance Monitoring
8. Concurrent Re-engineering	8. Worker-Driven Processes
9. Credibility Passion	9. Fear-Free Environment
10. Sensible Management	10. Supportive Culture

IMPERATIVE #1: COMMITMENT TO PURPOSE

This may sound to be old run-of-the-mill motherhood statement - but we found it exerting profound influence on the system acceptability and sustainability. Firstly, the following should be borne in mind regarding this entity:

- ▶ Purpose must be precisely defined and known to everybody concerned with that purpose.
- ▶ There should be a mechanism in place to exhibit tangible commitment to purpose.
- ▶ All purposes must be integrative - every smaller purpose must be accountable to a larger purpose, and all purposes must be accountable to the overall business plan.

Tangibly and unambiguously defining the purpose is important, or else people will keep asking you the question, "what is the purpose of this exercise" - and then you may be imparting different answers to the same question to different people at different times.

In a large government department where a new quality system was being implemented, because of a lack of well-defined purpose, you could hear the corridor murmurs, such as: nobody tells me anything - Oh! please, not another system - I think the system is only for the management - its another ploy to downsizing us - systems come and go, like all other systems it will die off its natural death. In a textile manufacturing plant where we were implementing the ISO 9000 system, the acceptance was very poor, because people were not given the reason, the purpose of why the ISO system is being implemented, what are its benefits, who is involved and how, etc.

IMPERATIVE #2: FUTURE SCANNING

One organization we encountered was fighting for survival - virtually on the brink of bankruptcy. The reason: they had no strategy for competitiveness. No greater vision for expanding their market share - they were only busy with their current customer base, which was also dwindling and shrinking. What they needed was continuous future scanning - to expand their customer base. To do that, we recommended that they should create a management group - a kind of think tank - to meet once a month, to brainstorm the future directions and strategies for the company. We also stressed that each manager must, at all times, wear two hats: a wish-hat and a must-hat. One for keeping a good control over the present operations, and the other to focus on long-term improvements.

As we indicated in earlier chapters, we believe that in the new millennium there will be a paradigm shift with regard to the meanings of "success" and "quality" - a new dimension will be added onto these entities - they will be eulogized to "competitive success" and "competitive quality".

IMPERATIVE #3: DYNAMIC CUSTOMER ORIENTATION

We have vociferously rallied around this motherhood statement for a long time - unfortunately, with a lot of yelp and very little action. It is virtually imperative to examine this entity vis-a-vis the following:

- ▶ Do we really know who our customers are?
- ▶ How do we exactly know what our customers want?
- ▶ Have we done enough future scanning to evaluate the needs of our potential customers?
- ▶ How have we **tangibly** shown to our customers that we care?
- ▶ Have we ever **tangibly** determined our customers' satisfaction level?
- ▶ What have we done dynamically, over and above the normal call of duty, to make our customers happy?

Take for example the scenario of a service organization - there are two basic rules that must be followed:

- ▶ Make sure that you allow "zero tolerance" on "attitude problems" for employees who directly come into contact with the customers.
- ▶ Make sure that you monitor the quality of your own service by becoming a client yourself.

IMPERATIVE #4: OPERATIONAL COMPETENCIES

To succeed, you have to grow. To grow, you have to have room to grow - which means, adequate infrastructural and operational competencies. You cannot expect people to make improvements, create excellence, or be motivated to outperform without proper tools, technology, and adequate support systems. For example:

- ▶ Infrastructural capability includes such things as: communication systems, transportational facilities, commercial facilities, adequate supply of energy needs, raw materials, technology, support systems, etc.
- ▶ Operational competencies include such entities as: state-of-the-art equipment, technology, processes, and materials, requisite procedures, logistics, and developmental means, adequate organizational and operational resources.

IMPERATIVE #5: QUALITY EXCELLENCE

This is indeed the most essential imperative, but also the most profoundly known and understood. Quality is success connection #1 - when everything else is equal in competition, quality provides the winning edge. Since this is the most crucial aspect of any business enterprise, we shall expound on this aspect at length in the next chapter.

IMPERATIVE #6: PERSONAL EXCELLENCE

This imperative relates to workforce motivation. Much has been said about this in the whole book. Motivation is, undeniably, the single most essential ingredient in the equation of success.

IMPERATIVE #7: CONTINUAL IMPROVEMENT MINDSET

An essential entity for growth, creativity, and excellence - in one organization, we implemented the following initiatives to accomplish this:

- ▸ Regular awareness and training sessions on continuous improvement
- ▸ Empowered teams for process improvement
- ▸ Tangible modes of recognition

IMPERATIVE #8: CONCURRENT RE-ENGINEERING

To explain this new paradigm - concurrent re-engineering - we have to narrate the state of our current practice of restructuring. Most companies continue to expend resources unchecked for years - suddenly things start getting out of hand - management wakes up to the fact - they start assessing the company's total operability framework: nature and extent of direct and indirect costs; optimization of resources - human/physical/financial; worker motivation; marketing strategies; profitability margins, etc. Now, the company starts to undertake profound restructuring and downsizing, as the only and most effective way of resolving the dilemma. The whole exercise creates a serious moral problem, causes disruption in the smooth flow of business, and causes extensive damage to the company in terms of productivity and market credibility. Intermittent actions such as these often do more harm than good. A further irony is that after the exercise is over, the organization once again quickly reverts back to its older routine of unchecked spending spree, and continues this modus operandi until its next craze for restructuring.

The solution to this and all other similar problems - "concurrent re-engineering" - a process of slow, systematic restructuring on a continuum - a process of challenging and appraising our operability on a continuous basis - to keep a continuous vigil and control of our operations. By doing so, the organization can avoid the once-in-five-year exercise of drastic reorganization or downsizing, and also avoid the unwanted side effects of these processes. We have applied this concept in a very large manufacturing organization with excellent results.

IMPERATIVE #9: CREDIBILITY PASSION

Success requires an obsession for excellence - dedication to the cause - a passion for market credibility - to be the best, for the customer, employees, and the market.

IMPERATIVE #10: SENSIBLE MANAGEMENT

Sensible management means sensible management - a hands-on simple process of commitment to the basic principles and guidelines of management. This imperative is meant to summarize our discussion, and is, therefore, elucidated through the following set of principles of what we call "sensible management".

- ▶ **Shared Management:** In the highly automated self-driven environment of the new millennium, managers and workers would be indiffernetiable. Management bust remain an integral part of the hands-on operability at all times. Employees respect and value exemplary leadership. Lead and create more leaders.
- ▶ **Integrative Operability:** Stand-alone systems generally have a limited shelf-life. A precursor to sustainable success is the establishment of integratively interactive systems.
- ▶ **Self-Directed Systems:** Systems must be people-developed, people-driven, people-controlled, and people-managed.
- ▶ **Operational Simplicity:** Remember! Operational procedures and documentation are meant to simplify things - not make them complicated. Continuously endeavour to simplify the operational infrastructure.
- ▶ **Continuous Training:** Training - a proven miracle ingredient in the recipe for success.
- ▶ **Process Improvement Focus:** Quality cannot be inspected-in - it has to be infused into the product piece by piece, process by process, through continuous process improvement.
- ▶ **Performance Monitoring:** The power and usefulness of any process or system can only be fully realized through a continuous monitoring and evaluation of its performance.
- ▶ **Worker-Driven Processes:** Create an infrastructure of teams and give people the pleasure and pride of controlling the processes that are theirs anyway.
- ▶ **Fear-Free Environment:** Give people the sense of self-discipline to create and innovate.

▸ **Supportive Culture:** For systems to succeed, two types of supportive impetus is fundamentally essential - management support, and cross-functional peer support.

CONCLUSIONS

For business success, think in terms of "totality, simplicity, and integration". Keep a close tab on the environment around you, continuously realign your operational framework with the ongoing market forces, learn from your experiences, establish a transparent working milieu, continuously monitor and reinforce your systems, empower people, and develop a value-adding culture. The shape of the successful organization in the new millennium, as we can see, would have the following attributes:

SHAPE OF A SUCCESSFUL ORGANIZATION
▸ Management is involved and committed. ▸ Organizational framework is flat and horizontal. ▸ Functional and operational operability is transparent. ▸ Organization is customer-driven. ▸ Constancy of purpose is a mandate. ▸ Quality excellence is a key focus. ▸ Working in partnership is a mission. ▸ Teamwork is a way of life. ▸ People empowerment is a commitment. ▸ Continuous improvement is an obsession.

Appendix B

TQBT: TOTAL QUALITY
BUSINESS TRANSFORMATION

INTRODUCTION

It is not our intent in this book to provide extensive discussion on the subject of quality and quality systems, because our main focus in this book is human business management, workforce motivation, and retention management. However, since quality excellence plays a very significant role in the overall equation for business success, we shall briefly outline the salient features of a good quality system, and provide some guidelines for developing such a system.

WHAT IS QUALITY

Let us first go over some preliminaries about quality. Quality has been defined in a variety of ways - some popular ones being:

Quality is   ... customer satisfaction
                 ... conformance to specifications
                 ... expression of craftsmanship
                 ... value for money

Personally, I prefer to define quality more in the human business management sense, as:

Quality = Mental Satisfaction

This simply means that, if you have created a certain level of quality with which you are satisfied, that is your level of quality. But, on the other hand, if you are still not satisfied, you would go on to undertake further improvements to create a better product or service. In this way, you will intertwine continuous improvement with your mental satisfaction to achieve excellence in quality. So really, quality improvement is a race without the finish line.

Notwithstanding, quality is a complex and multi-faceted concept. It is not a singular activity, or characteristic; nor a system or a department. Quality is the sum of all characteristics of a product or service that collectively contributes to its superiority and excellence. Consequently, there is no one single definition of quality. In fact, if you like, you can create your own definition of quality - vis-a-vis your own operational capabilities, your customer's perceptions and requirements, your culture - or anything else that you think impacts the perception about your products and services

THE AGE OF COMPETITIVE QUALITY

Rather than thinking of quality only in the context of your internal operability framework, today it would be more appropriate to define quality in a more interactive and global sense. Much like the paradigm shift of "success" to "competitive success" as we elucidated earlier, the norm of the day for quality is not only "quality", but "competitive quality". To clearly understand what this new requirement means, let us examine what "quality" has meant to us to date. Excellence in quality means:

- ▸ That, the product continuously meets the specified requirement.
- ▸ That, the vendor and the vendee are mutually agreeable on the price structure.
- ▸ That, the customer is satisfied with the delivery arrangements.
- ▸ That, the customer is satisfied with the service arrangements.

In today's marketplace, these quality characteristics can be virtually met by any producer. Where then lies the difference between a mediocre company and an excellent company? How does a customer identify and choose one company over another? That is where the new connotation of "competitive quality" comes into the picture.

Today's consumer is not the same as yesterday's. With enormous competitive availability of products and services, today's consumer has become extremely alert, intelligent, and demanding. They want higher quality goods at the lowest possible price - the best of both worlds. For the producers operating in an open and highly competitive global market-driven economy, these demands are virtually untenable, and yet the producers have to work hard to competitively meet these demands for success and survivability. The revised expectations vis-a-vis competitive quality, as a minimum, include the following:

Expectation of Buyers/Customers:

- The product should meet and exceed the specified requirements.
- Each piece, batch, or shipment should be consistently the same.
- There should be minimal or no price fluctuations.
- Delivery should be as per agreed upon schedule.
- Service should be prompt and dependable.

Expectation of Consumers/Users:

- The product should reflect the state-of-the-art technology.
- The product should be innovative in design and variety.
- The product should be competitively priced.
- The product should be fit for use.
- The product should be environmentally safe.
- The product should be user-friendly.
- The product should be value-adding.
- The product should exceed its intended life-span.
- The product should be serviceable with promptness.
- The product should provide a feeling of pride in its ownership.

Let us now summarize our findings - tomorrow's corporate boardrooms are going to be resounding with the echos of "competitive success" and "competitive quality". The prime determinant of competitive success is, indeed, competitive quality. Quality excellence, however, is a people-dependent phenomenon, and only a highly motivated and dedicated workforce can induce high levels of quality.

A final dictum!

Competitive Success = Excellence + Ethics

Competitive Quality = Quality + Value

QUALITY SYSTEM FUNDAMENTALS

How does an organization develop or select a suitable quality system? As was indicated earlier, the marketplace overwhelmingly abounds in quality improvement recipes, models, and systems. Any model is good as long as it appropriately accommodates the needs and infrastructural profile of the organization. My recommendation is that every organization should develop their own model that goes hand-in-hand with their existing systems, short-term/long-term goals, operational/functional/infrastructural capabilities and capacities, and the customer's needs. It is, of course, not to say that while developing your own model, you could not utilize the enormous wealth of knowledge and innovative ideas outlined in any or all of the existing systems, standards, philosophies, and methodologies propounded by well-known experts and gurus.

My personal experiences provide me with the testimony and strength to uphold the conviction that a self-developed, self-directed quality model has the greatest chance of lasting success. A self-developed model would have the following distinctive advantages:

- ► The ownership of the system will be in the hands of the people.
- ► People will be proud of it.
- ► The system will be compatible with the existing quality framework of the organization.
- ► It would make optimal use of available resources.
- ► It would be participatory, meaningful, value-adding, and understandable to everyone collectively.
- ► Overall, it would be a people-developed, people-empowered, people-driven, and people-owned system.

A successful system is, typically, one which has the ability to be adaptable and dynamic towards the market forces and demands. The global order is changing faster than we can comprehend. The impending environment of the year 2000 and beyond is going to be intensely competitive. Organizations are going to be experiencing greater challenges in terms of customer demands, better quality products and services, better designs, and competitive prices. What is tomorrow's customer looking for:

- ► Constancy in meeting or exceeding the specified requirements
- ► Constancy in batch-to-batch quality
- ► Constancy in pricing

- Constancy in delivery time
- Constancy in dependable service

Unfortunately, our present quality systems are grossly inadequate to meet the demands of the impending environment. Some of the basic deficiencies of our systems include:

- They are unintegrated and non-interactive.
- They are not proactively dynamic and are not flexible enough to adapt to the evolving demands and circumstances of the marketplace.
- Their scope is limited to short-term gains.
- They lack emphasis on people-management.

The impending environment of the year 2000 and beyond calls for something radically new and challenging - a total re-engineering and rejuvenation of our present quality systems - we are annotating it as "Total Quality Business Transformation (TQBT)". What is TQBT? It is a paradigm for success - an interactive whole system approach to business operability. The building blocks of the TQBT system are the following four pillars:

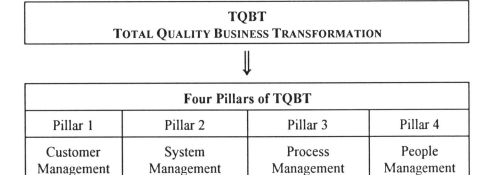

TQBT
TOTAL QUALITY BUSINESS TRANSFORMATION

⇓

Four Pillars of TQBT			
Pillar 1	Pillar 2	Pillar 3	Pillar 4
Customer Management	System Management	Process Management	People Management

BUILDING THE TQBT SYSTEM

It is extremely easy to build your own customized quality system, once you clearly understand what a quality system is and what does it involve. A quality system is not a tangible entity like a chair or a table, that you can buy in a ready-made package and bring it in to implement. A quality system is simply a collection of activities that you have to undertake to improve processes, which would then lead to the achievement of high productivity, good quality products and services, greater customer satisfaction, and ultimately, competitive success and profitability.

Obviously, therefore, in order to develop the system, the first step involves drawing-up a master checklist of all activities and processes required to be undertaken that impinge on the quality aspects of products and services. For a good quality system, this checklist must effectively accommodate, as a minimum, the following entities:

- Your own business plan, policies, goals and targets
- Market requirements and trends
- Customer demand and expectations
- Your current procedures, processes, and systems
- A profile of your operational and functional infrastructure
- Your technological capabilities
- Your production capacity and capability
- Your resource base

Next, you have to draw-up, for each process or activity, an action-item checklist - the things you have to do to undertake the activity or manage the process. Then, start integrating all these sets of actions into a coordinated plan so that an interactive whole system will emerge out of it.

With this understanding of the requirements of a quality system, we shall now proceed to outline the sequence of steps involved in the process of developing and implementing the TQBT system:

- Establish quality policies, objectives, and goals.
- Ensure that these goals are achievable and compatible with the overall business plan.
- Identify any requisite market constraints, trends, or demands that needs to be included in the quality plan.
- Establish a profile of customer requirements and expectations.
- Make a checklist of all activities required to be undertaken for the quality system.
- Draw-up an action-item checklist for each process or activity to be undertaken.
- Establish cross-functional interface to ensure that the system is interactive and integrated.
- Establish an appropriate responsibility framework.
- Allocate adequate resources.
- Provide requisite training to employees.
- Document and implement procedures.

- Ensure that everyone consistently follows the procedures.
- Measure and monitor process output.
- Establish procedures for evaluating system effectiveness.
- Continuously reinforce the system as required.
- Maintain emphasis on continual improvement.

FOUR PILLARS OF TQBT

Let us now build our action-item checklist of activities that needs to be undertaken for implementing the quality system. These are categorized under the following four headings:

- Customer Management
- System Management
- Process Management
- People Management

Pillar #1 : Customer Management

- Dynamic/proactive customer orientation process
- Customer consultative process
- Organizational commitment identification process
- Customer service procedure
- Customer feedback process
- Customer satisfaction determination process

Pillar #2: System Management

- Quality mission/vision
- Quality policy/objectives/goals
- Management commitment
- Responsibilities/authority/accountability
- Procurement/material control
- Quality system documentation
- Training/development
- Quality plan
- Design control
- Production control
- Cross-functional interface process
- Team management
- Quality records/reports
- Quality system auditing

- ▸ Servicing procedures
- ▸ Quality cost control
- ▸ System performance review
- ▸ Marketing control
- ▸ System sustainability control

Pillar #3: Process Management

- ▸ Procedure implementation control
- ▸ Process control
- ▸ Process verification/validation control
- ▸ Non-conformity control
- ▸ Corrective/preventive action procedure
- ▸ Document control
- ▸ Maintenance control

Pillar #4: People Management

- ▸ Employee Empowerment
- ▸ Motivation enhancement program
- ▸ Employee feedback process
- ▸ Employee complaint resolution process
- ▸ Employee recognition process
- ▸ Employee health/safety program
- ▸ Employee opportunity program

Now, for each of the system elements appended above, identify the following:

- ▸ Parameters affecting the elements
- ▸ The current best of the elements
- ▸ Things to be done
- ▸ Who will do it?
- ▸ What resources are required?
- ▸ What is the time schedule?
- ▸ How would it be controlled?
- ▸ What new initiatives are required?

The road map for implementing the TQBT is summarily encapsulated in the following TQBT axioms.

TOTAL QUALITY BUSINESS TRANSFORMATION
TBQT Axioms
1. Confirm management commitment 2. Develop customer/market profile 3. Evaluate current systems 4. Develop in-house customized interactive systems 5. Document the system 6. Establish implementation road-map 7. Focus on training and development 8. Implement operating procedures 9. Establish Process management teams 10. Evaluate process performance 11. Reinforce the systems continously 12. Continue total quality business transformation

The process of TQBT implementation as outlined in the above table is virtually self-explanatory. For each activity, a set of actions have to be identified, implemented, and maintained. We would like to emphasize here that the sustainability of the system can only be guaranteed if:

- The system is completely interactive and integrated.
- There is continuous cross-functional interface between design, production, process control, and customer service.
- The process control function is under the direct supervision of the empowerment teams.
- All procedures are properly documented and continuously reviewed/revised, as required.
- Procedures at all levels of the organization are strictly followed.
- System performance reviews are done at regular intervals.
- The system is continuously reinforced with additional resources as per the needs identified through system audits and reviews.
- Management commits to continuous improvement emphasis.

PROCESS MANAGEMENT

The third pillar of the TQBT system - the process management - is the most important entity for continuous quality improvement. We would like to expound on this subject a bit further to present a simple formula for continuous process improvement. To improve the system, it is imperative to improve the individual processes, because a system is nothing but a collection of processes. To begin with, we need to develop a clear sense of direction with regard to the following:

- ▸ What needs to be improved?
- ▸ What is the current best?
- ▸ What is the goal?
- ▸ How would the goal be achieved?
- ▸ How would the achievement be measured?

The "PURI" Process Enhancement Wheel, as appended below, provides simple cyclic guidelines for continuous process quality improvement.

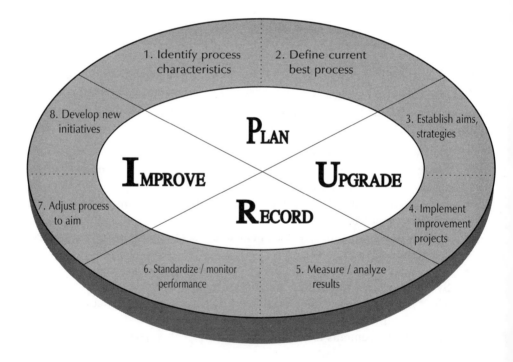

" PURI " Process Enhancement Wheel

A simple sequence of steps for process improvement are as follows:

PROCEDURE AND TARGET

- Identify the characteristics, variables, and attributes of the processes that need to be improved.
- Identify the state of its current level of excellence.
- Define a goal for enhancing each or all of the characteristics.
- Establish a strategy for implementing the improvement efforts.
- Identify improvement initiatives and projects.
- Implement the improvement plan.
- Monitor and control the improvement efforts.
- Identify deficiencies in the improvement initiatives.
- Take corrective and preventive action.
- Continue monitoring the performance.
- Evaluate results.
- Identify the improvements achieved.
- Standardize the achieved improvements.
- Adjust the process to the new standards and aims.
- Continue the cyclic process of improvement.

Appendix C

CHANGE MANAGEMENT

This chapter is devoted to the most important generic recipe for human business management - change management - a panacea for all diseases. Change management implies managing change in the organization effectively, so that it does not upset the smooth normal flow of business activity.

Change, in one form or another, is almost an inevitable phenomenon in any organization. There is little or no escape from it. But at the same time, change is indispensable for circumventing and preventing stagnation. Most organizations are cognizant of this fact - they know that to succeed, they have to persistently disturb the present. With new demands, organizations have to think and act anew, be adaptable, and change or realign their strategies.

Notwithstanding, however, when change transpires, whatever its nature, magnitude or need, it affects everyone in the organization, to a lesser or greater degree. The working levels generally bear the greatest brunt of change. And when that happens, all aspects of their operability becomes vulnerable to deficiencies. Thus, to understand and effectively manage the change process, we have to make the following enquiries:

- ► Why does change occur?
- ► When it does, what impact does it have on the behaviour patterns, motivation, and productivity of the workers?
- ► How can we neutralize or minimize the negative impact of change, and make the change process work for us, rather than against us?
- ► What is the management's role in managing change?
- ► What are the individual worker's responsibilities and contributions to the change process?

ANATOMY OF CHANGE

Whenever an organization initiates change, it does so for a valid and compelling reason - whether they relate to: financial, technological, competition, productivity improvement, customer demands, or market pressures. Organizations are not crazy to introduce changes for the fun of it - they are compelled to do so for survivability and success. The change process can culminate into either a minor readjustment, reshuffling, or re-engineering, or a major overhauling, restructuring, or downsizing. Depending on how change is managed, minor changes may or may not create any significant impediments in the flow of business operability. However, radical irreversible structural changes must be carefully handled, because they can polarize the organization, creating high levels of fear, anxiety, uncertainty, and demoralization of the workforce that can be damaging to the organization's health.

Change generally portrays two distinctly different facets - positive and negative, as follows:

FACES OF CHANGE	
Face 1: Positive	**Face 2: Negative**
► Opportunity ► Growth ► Progress ► Innovation ► Rejuvenation ► Success	► Unpredictability ► Upheaval ► Disorientation ► Instability ► Threat ► Disempowerment

Notwithstanding the nature or magnitude of change, most change processes are characterized by behavioural changes of some sort or the other. Generally speaking, an individual goes through some or all of the following stages of behavioural changes during the process of change:

1. Apprehension
2. Denial
3. Anger
4. Negotiation
5. Resentment

6. Depression
7. Cognitive Dissonance
8. Compliance

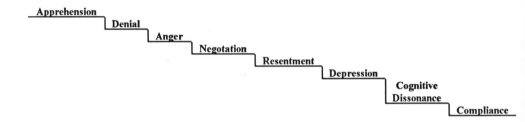

What is fundamental to change management is the ability of the organization to short-circuit these stages and achieve an individual's unequivocal acceptance as early as possible. The process of managing organizational change is a complex subject, and needs to be tailored specifically to the particular situation, culture and people who are affected by the change. Any good change management strategy assesses why individuals resist change and tailors a strategy to address each factor.

Change is a people-dependent phenomenon. Change brings about cognitive dissonance (psychological turmoil). For change to be accepted wholeheartedly, people must perceive a congruence among their feelings, beliefs and behaviour. Real change occurs only from the integrated personality of the person. Managers must be sensitive to the value system of the individual to bring about effective and lasting change. For this, the management must provide appropriate support systems that are congruent with the behavioural stages of change.

The major task in any change process is overcoming resistance to change. Different people react differently to change. Each person sees the change through a personal crystal ball. Some of the basic reasons why people resist change are as follows:

- ► Change represents unpredictability. It inculcates a fear of the future. People resist change not because they love the past, but because they are uncertain of the future.
- ► When change is not born out of the shared vision, people do not perceive a congruence between their beliefs and the nature of change.
- ► Change means giving up something - foregoing the familiar, snugly routine.
- ► Change implies instability, disorientation and loss of control.

▸ Most people consider change to be unnecessary, ill-conceived and detriment to the interests of the organization.

COGNITION AND CHANGE

In an earlier chapter, we elucidated the role of cognition in attitude formation and motivation. Cognition affects the change process in almost exactly the same manner, because the acceptance or rejection of change is also a direct resultant of an individual's attitude and behaviour towards change. The way an individual would perceive a situation, make a mental picture and draw conclusions, would determine how he would react to organizational change. Our thoughts, attitude and behaviour patterns can cause us to resist, or it can cause us to embrace and support the change. When change transpires in an organization, each person attempts to seek as much available information as possible about the situation. The cognitive faculties evaluate this information against personal needs, value systems, experiences, and fears, and draws conclusions about the validity and receptiveness of change. If there is a high degree of compatibility between a cognitive perception and beliefs, we shall formulate a positive mindset and behavioural stages of change would move faster towards acceptance of change. Many a times, of course, our judgements are biased in favour of our own interests. It's human nature to filter the information, through selective perception, in a personal way and draw conclusions that reflect our own viewpoint.

The magnitude and power of cognitive processes have a phenomenal impact on events. Just imagine how many different ways an individual can draw his or her own conclusions in a change process:

▸ If the available information is insufficient or unreliable, the individual's cognition is bound to make faulty assumptions.
▸ If there is a lack of operational transparency vis-a-vis the change process, the individual will formulate a sense of distrust, fear, and uncooperativeness.
▸ Even if the available information is reliable, the cognition can draw faulty assumptions and misinterpretations because of some preconceived emotional reactions and would, consequently, develop a negative mindset.

Undoubtedly, therefore, the speed at which an individual will accept change is highly dependent on the judiciousness and efficacy of his cognitive evaluations and emotive reactions to change. For change to be accepted wholeheartedly, both the individual as well as the manager have an important role to play. The manager must provide meaningful input about change and be sensitive to the value system of the individual. The individual must also endeavour to formulate unbiased and realistic evaluation of the total change process and must perceive a congruence between his perceptions and feelings.

MANAGERS AS CHANGE AGENTS

From the above discussion, let us draw some fundamental conclusions about the change process, as follows:

- ► Change is inevitable and indispensable.
- ► During the process of change, people go through a variety of behavioural changes.
- ► Attitude to change is a resultant of an inter-play between cognitive processes and emotional feelings.
- ► Acceptance of change comes through a clear understanding of the change process, balancing of cognitive and emotive reactions, and developing a positive mindset.

What role can the management play in facilitating the change process? Change can be brought about quickly and harmoniously, but it requires management's ingenuity, patience and dedication. Effective change management starts with understanding the process of change, identifying the factors that impact the change process, and developing suitable framework to facilitate the change process.

As a first step, organizations should endeavour to bring about change in a slow and systematic manner. Sudden and drastic changes create confusion, fear, apprehension and resistance. For instance, neither sudden empire-building is a wise strategy when profits are up, nor drastic downsizing is a panacea for all ills during market volatility and declining profits. Functioning under vacillating and inconsistent operational framework can rarely bring sustainable success. Constancy and stability are the most powerful tools for effective change management.

Secondly, it must be understood that change is a people-dependent phenomenon. Most people perceive change to be a negative entity. Change cannot be brought about by dictate. Compliance by dictate only brings about short-lived and cosmetic change. Real change occurs only from the integrated personality of the person. Consequently, organizations must clearly understand the needs, expectations and cognitive value-system of the people and develop appropriate framework to facilitate the acceptance process. The basic requirements of people during a change process can, typically, be characterized as follows:

- ► Clear picture of the change process

- ▸ Complete, reliable information
- ▸ Transparency of operations
- ▸ Cognitive Congruence
  - Unbiased, realistic evaluation of change process
  - Congruence with emotional feelings
  - Affinity with needs, expectations and beliefs
  - Positive attitude
- ▸ Management Support
  - Encouragement, support for personal role change
  - Maintenance of control, responsibility
  - Appropriate resources, opportunities
  - Involvement and empowerment
- ▸ Personal Growth
  - Personal suitability/capability for mid-course correction
  - Cross-functional interface impact
  - Long-term impact of change on personal growth

Finally, effective planning is fundamental to change management. Organization should not start swinging at the task of change without proper planning. Some of the essential elements of planning include the following:

- ▸ Identification of means of effective dissemination of information
- ▸ Development of proper communication network
- ▸ Preparation of managers to handle change
- ▸ Involvement of employees in the change process
- ▸ Transparency of operational framework

ROAD MAP FOR CHANGE MANAGEMENT

- ▸ Develop a plan for the change process, to include:
  - Purpose of change
  - Type and nature of change
  - Magnitude of change
  - Areas/units subject to change
  - Time schedule for change
  - Impact of change on units/individuals
- ▸ Develop a profile of change process.
- ▸ Identify channels of dissemination of information.
- ▸ Select and prepare capable managers to handle and coordinate the change process.

- ► Provide training to managers, if necessary, on behavioural aspects of human undertaking.
- ► Establish groups and encourage group discussions on the change process.
- ► Involve everyone in the change process.
- ► Clearly identify: nature of change; impact; benefits to the reorganization and individuals.
- ► Managers should utilize cognitive approach to change management and identify:
  - What information is available to the individuals?
  - How the individuals perceive the change process?
  - What are the individual's emotive reactions?
  - How does the individual evaluate the change process?
  - Is the change process compatible with the individual's beliefs and expectations?
  - What are the individual's perceptions about the long-term impact of change on the organization as well as himself?
  - What judgements and attitude the individual is forming about the change process?
- ► Managers should help individuals, in every possible way, to make the transition as smooth as possible.
- ► Develop a step-by-step plan for implementing the change.
- ► Develop a suitable infrastructure.
- ► Identify and provide the requisite resources.
- ► Monitor progress.
- ► Review/revise/reset priorities.

Making change happen seems awfully difficult. Sometimes it seems to take forever; sometimes it does not happen. In fact, the more successful the organization, the more difficulty it has changing. To turn around a negative change into a propitiously positive proposition, a manager must know when to implement a change, how much and how. In addition, managers must exhibit commitment, dedication and exemplary working attitude and behaviour towards change. More succinctly speaking, managers must act as change agents.

INDIVIDUALS AS CHANGE AGENTS

Although management plays a paramount role throughout the process of change, no amount of meaningful and sustainable organizational changes can transpire without an unqualified and unequivocal participation and acceptance of change by the individuals. Individuals can make substantial contributions in more than one of the following ways:

- ► Understanding the importance of change
- ► Alleviating any skepticism about the change process
- ► Assisting in implementing change with a positive mindset
- ► Becoming an instrument of change
- ► Becoming a change agent

The first most important thing for any individual is to understand the nature, reality and importance of change. Following are some of the essential elements of the change process:

- ► If the organization is instituting changes, it must be doing so for a good reason.
- ► Changes are not always a bad idea; changes also connote progress.
- ► Management has to make tough decisions to keep the company afloat.
- ► If the company is changing, the individual really has no choice but to change.
- ► Change does not come by easily; it brings with it difficulties, problems and disorientation.
- ► Management has neither all the answers, nor have the entire capability to make it happen. It's too big a job for the management to handle alone. They need your help.
- ► Individuals are also part of the organization and it is their duty to facilitate any process which the management deem important for the success of the organization. In fact, individuals are paid to handle problems, provide solutions and support the management. They are not paid to cause problems or resist the requisite changes.

We shall now append some guidelines on how individuals can make significant positive contributions to the change process:

- ► When changes transpire in the organization, try to be an active participant to the process.
- ► Seek reliable information and try to understand the true nature and impact of changes.
- ► Try to understand the organization's mandate and need towards the change process.
- ► Make a realistic cognitive evaluation of the changes.
- ► If the changes are for a worthy cause, try to develop a positive mindset and help facilitate the implementation process.
- ► If the changes are detrimental to the interests of the organization, present your viewpoint to the management and establish a positive rapport.

- ▸ Recognize and appreciate the managements's perspective:
  - Management has a specific responsibility towards the organization.
  - If changes are necessary, they shall have to be made. It's their responsibility to ensure that changes are implemented harmoniously and effectively.
  - Management have some idea how the changes will be implemented, but they don't have all the answers. They are themselves trying to discover the most optimal solution.
  - Change process is not the exclusive domain of management alone; it's everyone's responsibility.
  - Management, like anyone else, is also prone to making mistakes.
- ▸ Be tolerant of management's mistakes. Management is genuinely seeking your help. Instead of making their job difficult, try to help simplify the process and support management's efforts.
- ▸ Don't resist change. You can be singled out and accused of causing trouble and getting in the way of progress. Anger, frustration and resentment can offer no benefits.
- ▸ Consider change as a new challenge. Look for new opportunities in the change process. Expend your energies and efforts in making the change work rather than resenting and fighting the change.
- ▸ Grab hold of the opportunity and reinvent the future rather than redesigning the past.

"BE THE CHANGE YOU'RE TRYING TO CREATE."

MAHATMA GANDHI

About the Author

Subhash C. Puri is an internationally renowned author, lecturer, and consultant. He provides training and consultation on a wide variety of subjects such as: Business Process Management, Process Improvement, Workforce Motivation, Quality Systems, Project Evaluation, Retention Management, Performance Appraisal, Quality System Auditing, ISO 9000 and ISO 14000 certifications.

As one of the leading authorities on the subject of quality management, he has been a key note speaker and lecturer for many associations and organizations in several countries. For over 35 years, he has provided extensive training and consultation to numerous organizations and companies in the manufacturing, service, and public sectors at the national and international levels.

He has served as chairman and member of several ISO committees and has made significant contribution to the development of quality system standards. He has published extensively, including nine textbooks and numerous professional papers.

He lives in Nepean-Ottawa, Canada, and can be contacted at :Tel: 613-820-8407, or by Fax: 613-820-1739.

Other Titles by the Author

- ISO 9000 Certification and Total Quality Management, 2nd. Ed. (English, Portuguese)

- Stepping up to ISO 14000, Integrating Environmental Quality with ISO 9000 and TQM (English, Japanese)

- Statistical Process Quality Control - Key to Productivity

- Applied Statistics for Food and Agricultural Scientists

- Statistical Quality Control for Food and Agricultural Scientists

- Statistical Methods for Food Quality Management

- Statistical Aspects of Food Quality Assurance

INDEX

ORDERING INFORMATION

➜ **Order From:**

Capital Publishing
P.O. Box 30051,   250 Greenbank Rd.
NEPEAN, Ontario, Canada K2H 1A3
Tel: 613-820-2445;   Fax: 613-820-1739

➜ **Price Per Copy:**

- Canada: Can. $ 29.00 + Applicable Taxes
- USA/International: US $ 22.00

➜ **Shipping & Handling:**

- For first book: Canada: Can. $ 6.00; USA: US $ 5.00; International: US $ 6.00
- Add $ 2.00 for each additional book to cover Shipping/Handling

➜ **Payment:**

- Payable by check, to: Capital Publishing
- Orders from individuals, within Canada/USA, must be prepaid. Companies may prepay with a check; or fax or mail company purchase order - **Payment Due Upon Receipt.**
- International orders must be prepaid
- No returns allowed without prior arrangement
- Price subject to change without notice
- Volume Discount: 15% for orders of 10-30 books; 25% for more than 30 books

---

Also Available from the Publisher
(By the same author)

1. "ISO 9000 Certification & Total Quality Management", 2nd. ed. - 1995 (420 pp).

2. "Statistical Process Quality Control - Key to Productivity", 1984 (275 pp)

Note: For further details, please enquire.